Mrs Hilda May Phillips
For your 60th Birthday
Many Happy Returns.

Victor

SHEILA HOCKEN
Living with Dogs

To Hilda
Best wishes
Sheila Hocken

SHEILA HOCKEN
Living with Dogs

or How not to be a Failed Dog Owner!

LONDON
VICTOR GOLLANCZ LTD
1985

By the same author

EMMA AND I
EMMA V.I.P.
EMMA AND CO

For children

EMMA'S STORY

First published in Great Britain 1985
by Victor Gollancz Ltd,
14 Henrietta Street, London WC2E 8QJ

Copyright © Sheila Hocken 1985
All illustrative material © 1985 Bruce Waite
Published by arrangement with Sphere Books Ltd

British Library Cataloguing in Publication Data
Hocken, Sheila
  Living with dogs.
  1. Dogs—Training
  I. Title
  636.7'083   SF431

  ISBN 0-575-03551-X

Designed by BRUCE WAITE
Photography and illustration by BRUCE WAITE

Typeset by Rowland Phototypesetting, Bury St Edmunds, Suffolk
and printed in Great Britain by R. J. Acford, Chichester, Sussex

PREVIOUS PAGE *Sheila Hocken pictured with, from the left
Bracken, Mocha, Teak, Buttons and Katy*

CONTENTS

INTRODUCTION

The very first thing I can recollect from my childhood days is my mother shouting at me for stroking strange dogs. But I took no notice. I'd sit on the pavement and revel in the feel of their soft coats, and their cold noses against my hands. But my mother would always come and prise me away, lecturing me on the dangers of being bitten. My pleas to have a dog of my own were completely ignored. Although I didn't realise it at the time, my mother was afraid of dogs. Not only that, but we had our visual handicap to cope with. No one in the family could see further than the end of their nose and I am sure my parents felt that a dog around the house would only create another hazard.

I was seven years old when something happened to me that cemented my love of dogs for the rest of my life. I should, by rights, have been sent away to a special school for blind children, but my father had been sent away to school and my mother had been brought up in an orphanage, so they both felt that the family should stay together and, after much fighting with the Education Authorities, my mother persuaded a local junior school to accept me as one of their pupils. The walk to school each day wasn't too hazardous. As I couldn't see very far in front, I always looked down at the pavement, which was the best indication to me of kerbs and walls. It was the other children who caused me the biggest problem. Knowing I could hardly see at all, they would leap out from their gates and shout 'Boss-Eyed' at me, and my daily journeys could have become a nightmare if it hadn't been for one of the children's dogs. Each morning, she would come out to greet me, touching my hand with her cold nose and then pushing her soft, furry body against my leg and swishing her tail in the air. The little dog didn't care about my strange-looking eyes or how I found my way up to school every day with head stooped. She just wanted to be friends. She accepted me, without question, as a normal human being. Something the other children would never do.

I spent many a happy hour sitting and talking to neighbours' dogs, always longing for one of my own. Little did I realise then that a dog would change my whole life. At the age of nineteen, my vision had diminished to almost nil. I could just distinguish light from dark. My teenage years hadn't been a great improvement on schooldays. The visual handicap always got in the way. The few friends I had became engrossed in the opposite sex, something I was desperately afraid of. I never felt equal. I was almost ashamed of my blindness, until the day I met Emma.

I was advised by a Social Worker to apply for a guide-dog. I didn't need much persuading. And I still remember, with a tingling sensation of excitement, the moment I met Emma, the chocolate-coloured Labrador who was to change my whole way of life. We fitted together instantly like two halves of a jigsaw puzzle and I became a whole human being, with eyes, just like everyone else. The relationship between guide dog and blind person is totally different from that of a pet dog and owner. I had to put my whole trust and faith in a dog. So much so that I never thought of Emma as a dog, but a person, a mentor, a constant companion and friend.

I feel very fortunate that I have that relationship to call upon, for Emma taught me to respect the relationship between dog and human being. She retired from active duty at the age of eleven, after I had a successful eye operation, and although our relationship was never quite the same after that, it was still far closer than most people and their dogs. She left me with a need to work with other dogs, to have their companionship and love. A thirst so strong for canine company that I ended up with five dogs. There would be more if only we had the money and the space. Bracken and Buttons, two more chocolate Labradors, were the first to join us in 1978 and I set about their training with great enthusiasm.

Training the dogs was never any problem, it seemed to be an instinct I had. Talking to them also came as second nature and I soon learned to ignore passers-by on the pavement when they imagined I was talking to myself and not the little puppy I had on the other end of the lead. All this paid off. I realised that every dog had a capacity to learn the English language, if only they were given the opportunity. Simply training the dogs to be generally obedient as pets wasn't enough. I needed a working relationship, something special to aim for. I read every book about dogs and dog training I could lay my hands on, but always with the same results . . . great disappointment. The authors all appeared to approach dog training in a military, stiff and starchy manner. They lacked a sense of fun and adventure. Undaunted, I decided to join one or two of the local dog training clubs.

My introduction to one of these establishments chilled me to the very marrow. The village hall was packed with barking dogs and screaming human beings when I arrived for my first lesson. The trainer, a big, fat, untidy-looking woman, stood in the middle of the hall, handing out advice to the newcomers. I sat and watched, hoping to gain some valuable information. The first girl stood up with a border collie to tell the trainer that whenever she took her dog out on the lead he constantly jumped up to bite at her hand.

'Wear thick gloves,' the trainer told her with great confidence.

'Will that stop him?' the girl asked.

'No, but he won't be able to bite you if the gloves are thick enough, will he? And,' the trainer added, 'hit him on the head hard whenever he does it.'

Before I could actually believe what I was hearing, the next person stood up.

'I can't get my dog to retrieve,' she told the trainer. 'He keeps dropping the dumb-bell.'

'Oh, that's easy,' the trainer told her. 'Put the dumb-bell in his mouth and then bandage his mouth up for ten minutes every day so he can't drop it. That'll cure him.'

At that point, I realised this training club was definitely not for me and went home before I could hear any more insults to the canine brain. I was determined to keep searching to find people who loved and respected their dogs as I did. Who talked to them and treated them as friends, not some uncontrollable beast who must be beaten into submission on the end of a chain collar. The more I learnt of the methods of dog training used, the more shocked I became. The advice I was given by so-called dog trainers was contrary to my beliefs. Their methods and approach to a dog was so antiquated, I ceased to wonder at all the problem dogs I met every day in the park.

A dog should never be trained until it's six months old, I was told. Let them have their puppyhood out first. From what I'd seen, at six months old a dog was so out of hand it was almost impossible for the average owner to train it without reverting to a check-chain and brutal methods.

'You'll spoil that dog,' one trainer told me after he'd seen me reward Bracken with a chocolate drop. 'You shouldn't give dogs titbits, you should make your dog do as he's told without bribing him.'

I believe dogs should receive plenty of reward, whether it be titbits or praise, or just playing for a moment with his favourite toy.

'Dogs should be kept outside in a kennel,' I was informed by yet another authoritative dog trainer. 'They shouldn't be allowed in the house. They're only dogs you know.'

I cringed at the very thought of Bracken, Buttons and Emma living outside in a kennel. I know that's not the way to treat a dog. How can you possibly understand and train your dog if he's not accepted in the house as one of the family? My years with Emma taught me to understand how the canine brain works and that the best type of relationships are built through constant companionship and mutual understanding. I base my belief that a puppy can be trained at the tender age of six weeks on the methods used by the Guide-Dogs for the Blind Association, who send their puppies out, where possible, to the puppy walkers at the age of six weeks. A vast amount of research has been put in over many years by the Guide-Dogs for the Blind Association in discovering the puppy's most responsive time for going to a new home and receiving training. Puppy walkers do not train a dog in actual guiding work. This is done when the dog returns to one of the Guide-Dog Training Centres at around a year to eighteen months of age. But the puppy walker has the responsibility of training the potential guide-dog in all aspects of family life. First of all, to be clean in the house and then to be generally obedient and well mannered. Then to be accustomed to every type of situation the dog could meet as a guide—railway stations, buses, roadworks, etc., so that, by the time the dog is old enough to take the responsibility of a guide, he is well grounded in the everyday situations of living with a family. If you embark on your puppy's training at the tender age of six weeks, by the time he reaches six months he will be well behaved and a pleasure to be with. But, to do this, you must forget all the old wives' tales and approach your dog's training in a completely different manner. Every lesson should be filled with enthusiasm and fun and a desire, on your part, to teach your new puppy as much as possible. I believe the more you teach your puppy the more intelligent he will become.

Dogs are very similar to people in the respect that their aptitudes and abilities to do various things are different. Not all dogs could be guides, or herd sheep, or win first prizes in Obedience shows, but every dog has a far greater capability of learning than most owners realise. Emma taught me never to underestimate her capacity for learning the names of shops and routes to various places and she made me realise that dogs have a great deal of reasoning power, if only they are given the opportunity to use it. Bracken furthered my education tremendously in understanding dogs.

When Bracken's basic training was complete, I had every intention of embarking on a show career with him in the Obedience world but my first try at winning a class was thwarted by Bracken. Once in the ring he acted the fool and made it quite clear to me that this was definitely not his vocation in life. I took the time to study him a little closer and try and gain more understanding of what he would be best at. It became obvious that what Bracken enjoyed most was entertaining people. He learnt all the new things I then began to teach him with great enthusiasm. He learned to bark on command, to yawn, growl and retrieve anything—including an egg without cracking it. I could have persisted and made Bracken work in the Obedience ring, but that is not my way. Instead, I found a dog who would enjoy the obedience life: a little black Labrador called Katy, who revels in her visits to dog shows and leaps up and down with joy at the mention of heel work. I have tried to teach her some of the things Bracken has most enjoyed doing but she's not at all interested and shows no desire to bark or yawn on command.

The most important thing in any relationship is compatibility. You are going to live with your dog for the next ten to fifteen years. It is naïve to think that you can buy any puppy of any breed and any temperament and live together happily. When I applied for a guide-dog, I was amazed at the care that was taken to match me to a dog. Height, weight and speed of walking are all very relevant to a guide-dog and owner but voice control, my way of life, my hobbies, my likes and dislikes were also taken into account. I was then put on the list to wait for a suitable dog. On reaching the training centre I had to wait two days for the trainer to assess me and the dog he'd chosen, to be absolutely sure we would match each other. My life depended on being united with the right dog. In those two days, our trainer told us all about dogs. How to feed them, groom them, exercise them and generally to care for them and we were also introduced to Fred. Fred was a life-size, plastic model, guide-dog. The trainer spent some time instructing me on how to give commands and praise to Fred. In retrospect, I'm sure it was a very amusing sight to see me praising and patting a plastic dog. But I had to get it right. My very future depended on it. I spent a whole month at the Guide-Dog Training Centre learning how to be a responsible dog owner. Although all the guide-dogs are fully trained, the owners aren't and no dog will work for a human being unless there's love and respect on both sides. Every blind person has a month to gain that dog's respect. They all do. Every blind person puts their heart and soul into loving and respecting their dog. Consequently, a beautiful relationship blossoms.

I hope this book will prove to you the whole relationship is based on choosing the right puppy. Dogs vary in their temperament enormously, as do human beings. Therefore, it is the most sensible approach to find a puppy with the temperament that suits you. You will have no training problems if you and your dog are suitably matched and you begin your training early enough, with the correct attitude of mind.

Sheila Hocken.

SHEILA HOCKEN
Stapleford, 1984

CHAPTER 1

CHOOSING
THE RIGHT PUPPY

Choosing a puppy appears to be rather a haphazard affair, and when you consider how many different breeds there are to choose from and how human nature varies, it's not surprising we sometimes end up with the wrong dog. So, let's approach the subject of buying a puppy from a completely diffent angle—the puppy's. For a long-lasting and fruitful relationship, you need not only the right breed, but also the right temperament. First of all, we must sweep away all the old sayings about buying dogs: for example, if you have a large house you can have a large dog; if you live in a flat you must have a small dog. As far as I am concerned, the size of your living accommodation is irrelevant to the size of your dog. A Great Dane will be quite contented living in a flat if he's given the right amount of exercise and attention from his owner, and let's forget the nonsense about little dogs requiring little exercise. Unless you're thinking in terms of a Chihuahua, every dog needs to be exercised daily.

The problem with most prospective owners is that they don't consider that their life style has any relevance to the dog they choose. They don't stop for one moment to think of their own temperament and ability. Choosing a dog should be just as important as choosing a husband or wife. After all, you're going to live with each other for the next ten to fifteen years. I know that if there's a particular breed you have your heart set upon I will not be able to change your mind; I just hope it's the right choice. And for those of you who are in a quandary, let me give you a few guidelines.

Are you fit to own a dog?

Your temperament, physical fitness, height, weight and wage packet should all come into your considerations. Let's take it from the bottom. The wage packet is important in the size of dog you can afford to feed. The days of feeding the family pet on scraps have long since gone. A large breed of dog, such as a German Shepherd (Alsatian) or Doberman, will eat about

*Do not make a mistake when choosing
your puppy or he could end up behind bars*

two pounds of food a day whereas smaller breeds, such as Yorkshire terrier and toy poodle, will only require four to six ounces. Then, there's the strength of your body and mind to consider. I have seen a four-month-old Great Dane puppy drag his owner along the pavement. I have also seen a 6′ 2″ man with a voice like thunder endeavouring to persuade his Yorkshire terrier that he is not an ogre.

Are you able-bodied and fit enough to cope with the demands of dog ownership? It's no good complaining, 'The old leg hurts,' when the dog's desperate to go out for a walk.

Can you be completely honest with yourself about your temperament? If not, ask your nearest and dearest to assess it for you. I don't wish to cause a rift in any marriages, but it won't do the dog a lot of good if you lie to each other.

Are you short-tempered and ready to fly off the handle at the least opportunity? If so, what will you do when your new puppy has chewed the leg off your Chippendale? Are you placid and good-natured, finding it hard to reprimand the kids when they tear the place to shreds? Would you mind dog hairs in the lounge and muddy paw marks across your kitchen floor? Will you be prepared to give up some of your telly-watching to pay a little bit of attention to your dog?

In all honesty can you offer a dog a decent home? I don't mean that you should have a palatial mansion with a three-acre spread; not at all. A dog needs human companionship more than he needs material assets. But you must be practical. If you live in a flat, fine, but *do* you have somewhere to exercise the dog? Can you really face carrying puppy up and down six flights of steps, ten times a day for him to be a 'busy dog' on the grassy bit outside? Many blocks of flats do not even have a piece of ground available for your puppy to relieve himself. You must consider this. It would be very unfair to take on the responsibility of dog ownership, and then realise there is nowhere to exercise him. I feel very strongly that people who live in cities and flats should be entitled to dog ownership just like everyone else. We are not all lucky enough to own a house with a garden, and I spent many years in flats in the middle of a city with a dog. But it does mean extra hard work. You must be sure there is somewhere your puppy can relieve himself regularly—not on the public pavement. I am very sorry that there are people who allow their dogs to foul the footpaths, because these people get all dog owners a bad name. With a little extra effort the city owner can be just as conscientious a dog owner as anyone else. Be sure there is somewhere nearby to exercise the dog off the lead—a park, woods, fields, but definitely not a children's play area. Imagine a cold November night, pouring down with rain, and that your allotted dog exercise area is half an hour's walk away. Will you really be prepared to drag yourself away from the television and the central heating to give your dog the exercise he needs and deserves?

What type of dog will best suit you?

Having answered all these questions, you will know whether you still want a dog or not, and can now turn your attention to the type of dog which would fit in best with you and your way of life. Don't just look at the different breeds of dogs. Do a little research into their background and what they were originally bred for. This will give you a far better idea of the temperament your dog will grow up with. But beware, reading all the different breed books can be a trap. Every breeder will be tempted to tell you of the virtues of his favourite dog. Not many of them will tell you of their faults. Obviously, I can't go through every breed for you here, but I will try to take a cross-section, to show you what you're looking for.

The Labrador, the dog I am most familiar with, was bred to retrieve game birds. Therefore, he's been bred to sit steady to the sound of gunfire, go out quietly and retrieve and to return to his owner. Nevertheless, he's a very active dog and can work an eight hour day in the field and still look as fresh as a daisy: so he will want plenty of exercise. Here I can tell you how to read between the lines and find the faults of the breed. Living with Labradors for many years, I am familiar with many of these. Retrieving is an instinct, and your Labrador may not care what it is he fetches for you, whether it be a cushion off the settee, a towel off the rail, a slipper from upstairs (which will probably be half-chewed by the time you receive it), or more unmentionable, horrible things he'll find and bring back to you in the fields. Within the same category you could consider the poodle—although for show purposes he is no longer regarded as a gun dog. It is a great shame that people look upon him now as a coddled pet, because he was originally bred to retrieve game from water and can be a very intelligent, active dog.

I can speak from personal experience of the poodle's temperament and characteristics, as when I was living at home with my parents I managed to persuade them, after pleading for five years, to let me have a dog and our first one was a miniature poodle. But I made a big mistake—not in buying the dog, but where I bought her from—a pet shop. I am sure we paid around double the going price: she cost us eighteen guineas back in 1960. The pet shop alleged that she had been innoculated against everything, but at the tender age of five months we lost her with distemper. In that short time she proved to me that poodles are much more intelligent than most people give them credit for. They are extremely quick to learn and can weigh up the temperament and characteristic of their owner immediately. As a breed I would say that they do not suffer fools gladly and will take advantage of a stupid owner to get their own way. As well as being intelligent and quick to learn they have the great advantage of not shedding their coat all over your furniture. But, remember, they need clipping frequently and this can be an added expense, unless you can turn your hand with a pair of clippers.

Our poodle cost us such a lot of money, not only to buy, but in vet's bills too, that when we lost her we were not able to afford to buy another one, which was what I really wanted.

Instead, we had a boxer who was going cheap as her previous owners had not been able to handle her. Peggy, as she had been christened, was a completely different type of dog from our poodle. She hit our little home like a whirlwind, showering us with love and affection. My mother was instantly afraid of Peggy. She wasn't used to big dogs bombarding her with paws and kisses. But, contrary to belief, Peggy loved my mother and didn't take advantage of her because of her fear. She would have laid down her life for my mother, she worshipped her so much. Although she was very attached to one person in the family, she loved everyone and would never settle in the evening unless all the family were at home around her. Boxers are extremely boisterous and very wilful, but having said that they are not the type of dog to take advantage of a less intelligent owner. They are more likely to take them under their wing and become a mother figure to the family. In my opinion the potential boxer owner should be full of life and exuberance and have plenty of patience where training is concerned.

The collie and sheepdog varieties were, of course, bred to herd sheep, and this category includes the German Shepherd who is, as his name states, a sheepdog. The sheep herders will need a tremendous amount of exercise, not only for their bodies, but for their brains. They are very quick-witted dogs and are happier living with a quick-witted person. I might add here that I am perfectly honest with myself and know that I am not nearly fast enough to live with one.

The hound group were bred specifically to hunt, either by sight or smell. You cannot ignore the overriding instincts in any breed and in the main a hound will want to hunt. For example, the beagle, which is quite a nice, neat size and very sweet-tempered, is often taken for a family pet, regardless of the fact that this dog loves hunting. Many pet owners I have spoken to have had problems because their beagle has found a way out of the garden and gone off on his own. Beagles do make lovely family pets because they do have such an easy-going temperament, but be sure you have a well-fenced garden and you are prepared to spend some time giving your dog the freedom he deserves. On the subject of the hound group, I am surprised that there are not more greyhounds kept as pets. This is probably because they are viewed as purely racing animals, but I have known quite a few racing greyhounds that have made an ideal family dog. Around the house they are very quiet and easy to train, and contrary to expectations I have never seen a greyhound pulling on the lead. They appear to save their energy for the few minutes they can gallop in open countryside.

The terriers were also bred to hunt, but in a different way. They were used when the game had gone to ground—rabbits, hares, etc. All the terriers

I have met are bursting with energy and a zest for life. These type of dogs will want to be on the go, whether it be in the fields looking for mice or in the home looking for something to do, and a bored dog is just like a bored child. Leave them to their own devices and they will be noisy and unruly. Educate them and spend time with them and they will become intelligent and controllable.

Every breed of dog was bred for a special purpose, whether it be retrieving, hunting, guarding, herding and, in the case of some toy varieties, just as a companion for man. You should keep this in mind, for however long ago the breed was used for its job of work, there is bound to be a little of that instinct left. A terrier will be in his seventh heaven rootling around woods for hours on end. A gun dog will be in his element retrieving for you, whether it is a dead bird or a rubber ball. It would be cruel to keep one of the sheepdog varieties without giving him something to occupy his active brain and it would be silly of you to buy a breed that was originally bred for guarding and then be annoyed when he did his job—even if it was on the milkman.

Where to buy your puppy

Now, after many weeks of burning the midnight oil reading all those breed books, where do you go for your puppy? What breeders can you rely on? The best advice I can give you is to ask your local veterinary surgeon, who will give you an unbiased opinion of who he thinks is the best breeder in your area. In my experience, the best puppies come from those breeders who only keep a small number of dogs and have the occasional litter. These people are far more involved with their puppies and take great care in their welfare. The larger kennels who breed quite a selection of different types and rely on staff to care for the litters cannot possibly give the necessary time and attention to each litter.

Don't be afraid to shop around. If a breeder does not want you to look at his puppies until you've ordered, then go elsewhere. You're looking for clean, healthy puppies and a breeder who has the best interests of his dogs at heart. Those breeders who ask you no questions and take the money eagerly are to be avoided. The ones who give you a third-degree on how the puppy is to be housed and reared and trained are the best to buy from.

Which puppy?

Once you have settled on the breed you require and found a reliable breeder, you still have a lot of work in front of you before you can take the right puppy home. Ensure that you can have the puppy at six weeks old and that, in the meantime, the breeder will allow you to sit and watch the puppies at play. You can learn so much from seeing how their mother chastises them, from watching their rough-and-tumbles and how they bite each other and play together. For in the near future you are going to simulate these games with your puppy.

How can you choose the right puppy from the litter and be sure he'll match your temperament? 'Oh, but he'll choose me,' I can hear you say. The one who rushes out, climbing over brothers and sisters, dives on your foot and chews your shoelace is the one you'll pick. Probably your biggest mistake. That is the most dominant puppy of the litter. A far better way of assessing each puppy's character is to carry out the series of temperament tests I have listed below, between the age of five and six weeks. The breeder must do this, as the puppies will give a totally different picture if tested by a stranger. Each puppy must be tested individually, away from its mother and brothers and sisters, either on a quiet lawn or in a room in the house and, as each test is completed, write the correct number down on your list.

List of temperament tests

Test One: Place puppy on the ground. Walk away, calling him. If the puppy follows and tries to bite shoes and shoelaces, or hang on to trousers as the breeder walks, he belongs in category number 1. If a puppy follows joyfully, jumps up and doesn't bite, he belongs in category number 2. If he follows, but a little uncertain with tail down, put him under number 3. If he refuses to come at all, he's a number 4 puppy.

Test Two: Place puppy on the ground. Sit down on the floor a little way away. Call him, pleasantly, clapping your hands. If he comes and bites hands, he belongs in group number 1. If he comes and licks, wagging his tail, put him under number 2. If he comes uncertainly, he belongs in group number 3. If he refuses to come at all, he's a number 4 puppy.

Test Three: Make as much noise as possible, perhaps by banging a pan on the floor or clattering two pans together. If puppy rushes to see what the noise is and tries to attack the source, he belongs in group number 1. If he comes to see what's happening, but doesn't attack the source, he belongs in group number 2. If he's a bit wary and stands looking, not quite knowing what to do, he's a number 3. If he runs away and hides, put him in group number 4.

Test Four: Roll puppy on his back and hold him there. If he fights and bites, he's a number 1 puppy. If he fights but doesn't bite, he's a number 2. If his efforts are a little more feeble then he belongs in group number 3. If he lies there, totally accepting your dominance, he's in group number 4.

It is essential to play with your puppy if you want a happy and obedient dog

Test Five: Take puppy, with your finger and thumb, by the loose skin on the back of his neck, shake gently and use a slightly reprimanding tone. This is the action his mother will take when she's telling him off. She takes the flesh between her teeth and probably gives him a nip. There is no need to do that. Just a gentle shake will show well enough which group puppy belongs in. If he turns round to bite, he belongs in group number 1. If he ignores it and continues playing, he belongs in group number 2. If he stands a little unsure of himself and worried, he belongs in group number 3. If he runs away he's a group 4 dog.

Dog or bitch?

Finally, you must decide whether you want a dog or a bitch. In my opinion, the old saying that the dog is dominant and the bitch is loyal has no credence. If you are not interested in breeding, then the sex of your puppy is irrelevant if the temperament is right. If you have no intention of breeding from your dog, then I advise that you have him castrated or her spayed. The ideal age is around a year old, but I advise you to consult with your veterinary surgeon on this matter. I am astounded at the attitude of many male dog owners on my suggestion that they have the dog castrated. Their usual retort is, 'It's cruel. You're taking his natural rights away from him.' In my view, it is criminal to keep a male dog entire and never let him mate a bitch. These owners are asking their dogs to live the life of a monk. The entire male dog will be in constant search of a bitch and, therefore, suffer mental anguish. It is far kinder to have him castrated before he reaches full maturity. Bitches that are unspayed and constantly left to cope with their 'seasons' can also suffer a lot of mental anguish, with false pregnancies and milk. Eventually, the unspayed bitch usually develops womb problems that can often be fatal.

Much of what is said about the effects of spaying and castration of dogs is not necessarily true. Those owners who insist on keeping their dogs entire make excuses that their dogs will get too fat or idle. Any dog will become too fat if he is over-fed, and idle if he is under-exercised. All guide-dogs, male and female, are castrated and spayed and I have not seen many fat guide-dogs around. This is mainly because guide-dog owners are properly educated and trained before they are given a dog. What a shame the pet owner does not have to go through a month's intensive training before he or she is allowed to own a dog.

If you are thinking of breeding from your bitch or having your dog at stud, think carefully. Breeders are not going to flock to use your stud dog unless he has proved himself in his particular line, either in the show ring, obedience or trials. Having bred puppies and kept a dog at stud I can speak from personal experience. Bracken was kept entire until he was two-and-a-half, for the simple reason that he was chocolate, had a good pedigree and was in demand. But in the end I had him castrated for his own peace of mind. He lived with four other bitches and it was heartbreaking to see him pine when one of them came in season and I didn't want them to mate. There was no way I could keep one of the bitches or Bracken tied in a kennel when seasons occurred. They were all first and foremost my pets. Bracken still fraternises with the bitches, but of course it has taken his absolute urge away and he is a much happier and more contented dog. Breeding from your bitch is time-consuming, expensive and heartbreaking. I can't bear to part with my puppies when they are old enough to go to their new homes. Consequently I have bred very few litters. Teak, our German shorthaired pointer is spayed. Buttons, who has had three litters and is now seven, will be spayed soon, as my vet strongly advised me that if she is left to come into season as she gets older she will have more problems.

Almost every day I meet the problems of the entire dog. To put it mildly they are a nuisance. Often, when my dogs are going for a walk through the woods, we are followed by frustrated males, despite the fact that our bitches are not in season. What really annoys me is that the owners of these dogs usually blame me. 'You must have a bitch in season,' they accuse. In fact, one of these dogs who was a constant nuisance to me, finally showed himself up for what he truly was—a sex maniac! In the summer holidays Kerensa always comes with me to the park, and she likes to take her own dog—a stuffed one on wheels called Bicky. One day last summer, our sex-maniac dog was in the park with his owner, who always accused me of having a bitch in season. The dog took one look at Bicky and let fly. He leapt on the stuffed dog's back and proceeded to try and mate it. Being on wheels, Bicky catapulted across the grass, and the harder the male dog tried to mate it, the faster Bicky wheeled away—with the owner in hot pursuit, screaming obscenities about what she was going to do to her dog when she eventually caught him. My only comment to this irate owner, on retrieving Bicky, was that this dog was definitely not in season!

The Match

At this point, you could really do with a computer—the type used to set up marriages. You have masses of information on yourself and a litter of puppies, and you now need to sit down and work out which puppy's temperament best matches your own.

The puppies with the most 1s and 2s are the most dominant of the litter. These dogs will be brave and bold, afraid of nothing and no one, and if you are looking for a working dog or a guard dog, then these are what you are looking for. And remember your own temperament: if you too are forceful, bold and afraid of no one, this puppy will suit you admirably.

The puppies falling into categories 2 and 3 are the middle of the road and will suit you if you just want an ordinary pet and are a normal well-adjusted family.

The 3 and 4 puppy will be very submissive, probably shy and a little nervous. This puppy will suit you if you are quiet but prepared to give time and reassurance and plenty of patience when training.

It is most important for you to take into account that each breed varies. Some breeds are more dominant as a whole and many types are of a shy and retiring personality. For example, a Labrador with 3 and 4 marks will probably not be nearly as sensitive as a Shetland Sheepdog in the same category. Sensitivity or dominance are not bad things. These traits only become bad when they are wrongly matched and handled. Shetland Sheepdogs make wonderful working dogs, and are taking many prizes in the Obedience ring because they are sensitive to their owners' wishes. But handled by someone who is all yank and yell this type of dog could so easily be ruined. At the opposite end of the scale let us take a German Shepherd of the 1 and 2 characteristics. This type of dog makes a marvellous police dog as he is bold and brave. Dominance does not mean a dog will attack. A vicious police dog is useless. Instead they are trained not to attack but to restrain. The bold dog will need leadership, someone to respect and look up to. If you are a weak-willed, submissive person, this type of dog will definitely not suit you.

Who is suitable for what?

Below are a few examples of the type of dogs I feel sure will match various families.

Family Number 1: Family Number 1 live in a semi-detached house with an average-sized garden and two children. Both parents have never had a dog before but the unanimous vote is for a larger breed. Both parents are willing and able to exercise a large dog.

Considerations: A breed must be chosen that will be completely reliable with children and easy to train by inexperienced people. Both parents are of a stable and happy nature but the children, of course, are rowdy and bouncy.

If I were choosing a breed of dog for this family, I would give them a choice between an English or Irish setter, golden retriever or Labrador and rough collie. From here, I would ask the parents a few more questions. Are they prepared to take the time to groom a heavy-coated dog such as a rough collie? If not, that would be disqualified from the choice. If, on the other hand, the wife would enjoy grooming a dog, then this breed is the ideal family pet. At the other end of the scale, the Labrador, being smooth-coated, needs the least attention to his coat. A brush once or twice a week is quite adequate.

Having chosen the breed of dog they would prefer from this selection, I would advise this family to pick a dog with 2s and 3s from the temperament test.

Family Number 2: A husband and wife with no children, a large house out in the country and plenty of experience in handling dogs. Their requirements: first and foremost, as a guard and, secondly, as a companion to the wife. The smooth-coated breeds to choose from would be the Doberman and the Rottweiler, both excellent guard dogs. In the rougher-coat variety, the German Shepherd or one of the Belgian sheepdogs. And I would advise a puppy chosen from the 1s or 2s in the temperament test.

Family Number 3: An elderly couple or single elderly person requiring a small dog for companionship. If they are prepared to cope with a coat, a Yorkshire terrier or toy poodle is ideal. If not, then a short-haired dachshund or a Boston terrier. If the dog is required as an alarm—barking when anyone knocks at the door—then I would choose a more dominant puppy, the 1s and 2s. If required as purely a pet by someone who hasn't much experience, I would go to the 3s and 4s.

Be honest with yourself

The most important thing when choosing a puppy is that you must be honest with yourself in assessing not only your capabilities and physical fitness for dog ownership, but your character. The best way I can describe to you how to match yourself to a dog is to explain how I match with Labradors, and how various friends I know match with their breeds of dogs. I am going to try and be as honest with you as I can about my own temperament. Firstly, I am basically idle, so if I chose a breed with a heavy coat I am sure I would occasionally miss the daily grooming sessions. Although I love walking and being out in the country, the faster type of breeds would not suit me. I need a slower-moving dog who I can keep within my sight-range. I need a dog with an easy-going temperament, as that's how I view myself. For example, I might get a little annoyed that one of the Labradors has stolen my freshly-baked apple pie, but what's the use of ranting and raving, it won't bring the pie back. I suit admirably the basic idleness of the Labrador, who will more often than not get a comfortable place and curl up and snore for an hour or two while I sit in peace and read a book. There are many things that you may not like about the Labrador: their total greed to steal and eat anything, or their mania to retrieve. This habit of retrieving, or just carrying anything, is an endearing one to me, but would frustrate other people and I know that the easy-going, love anyone, temperament that most Labradors have would not suit everyone. Harold and Betty for instance, my husband's cousin and wife, who are also our closest friends, own a Weimaraner. Harold makes no bones about the fact that he thinks Labradors are disloyal, lack character, and are, as far as he's concerned, totally uninteresting dogs. Zelda, their Weimaraner, has a very different temperament from that of a Labrador. She worships Harold and Betty and is not in the slightest bit interested in other dogs or other human beings. I have a friend who owns border collies, and I find it very difficult to imagine her with any other breed. She is precise, quick-witted, full of energy and has that driving force for life that a few lucky humans possess. These two examples are of good matches. I know of plenty of bad ones. I know the original male chauvinist pig who bought himself the most beautiful German Shepherd puppy. At first, the puppy displayed all the characteristics of his breed, friendly, bold and keen to learn. After eighteen months of living with his chauvinistic owner he has changed completely. He has become just like his owner, aggressive and arrogant. But now the poor dog is suffering from these enforced characteristics and because he is so aggressive he is no longer given his free runs in the park as he has already attacked and maimed two dogs. Of course in an ideal world people like this would not even own a dog.

While you are trying to match yourself to a breed of dog, you should take into consideration your reasons for wanting a dog. My reason is plain and simple, I love dogs and I really don't think I could live without them. But there are all sorts of different reasons that make people go out and buy their first dog. Often it's because the children want one. If this is your reason you must consider the responsibility very carefully. No matter how old your children are you must be prepared to look after and train the dog yourself. Apart from the fact that your children will one day leave home and you will no doubt be left with the dog, if it is not a dog of your choice or you are incompatible then you may lead a very miserable life together. You may decide to buy your first dog after a spate of local burglaries. This puts you in rather a dilemma. A good house dog will need a dominant temperament and if you haven't owned a dog before this could cause you problems. In this situation it would be advisable for you to have a smaller dog that you know you can handle. After all, you only need a dog as an alarm, not necessarily to kill the burglar.

A sensible idea would be for you to put pen to paper and list your requirements for your ideal family dog. You can then make a check-list with each breed you fancy. For example, if your first and foremost requirement is that of a guard dog, you may as well cross the Labrador retriever, the golden retriever and the setters off your list. Often these dogs are quite good at barking at a stranger's approach, but just as often they don't bark at all. Your second requirement may be that a dog must be trusted with young children. Most dogs who are treated with respect by children and trained

Which puppy is right for you?

correctly can be trustworthy. In the cases that I have come across where dogs have bitten children, it's often because they have not been trained and are allowed to dominate the family, or the children have been very cruel and left to tease a defenceless puppy. You may choose your breed purely on looks. An example of this is the Afghan hound, which is an exquisite-looking creature. I have known and loved many Afghans, but they are a dog on their own. They tend to be aloof and act like aristocrats. They are not generally accepted as easily trainable, although I know they can be trained and be very responsive with the right person. But most of the Afghans I see now are either matted-up and filthy or have their coats clipped away so that the owner does not have to groom them. I cannot understand the desire to have a dog with a long coat which is then either left to mat or is clipped off. Probably prospective owners of Afghans, Old English Sheepdogs and the like do not realise or stop to consider the amount of time and effort that goes into keeping these dogs as beautiful as they should be.

As yet, I have given no mention to the mongrel, or cross-breed. The temperament test will work just as well on a litter of mongrels as it does on pedigree puppies. The sad thing is, mongrels are looked upon as the scum of the dog world by many people, but as far as I am concerned it is just as valuable as a dog as the very best pedigree. It doesn't matter what a dog looks like, it's what's inside that really counts. The majority of mongrel owners that I have come across have not chosen them from a litter but have either rescued them or brought them from one of the dog sanctuaries. Suiting yourself to an older puppy or adult dog can be a very different matter from choosing a puppy in a litter, so I have allotted mongrels a chapter of their own later in this book.

It is impossible for me to choose the right puppy for you without knowing all the facts. I can only put forward a few ideas and give a general guideline. The fact that I have advised some breeds as good guard dogs, does not mean that they are vicious or would not make ideal family pets. In the end, the choice is yours. Every puppy has the right family somewhere. Let's hope you both meet up.

Warning

Have you given enough thought and consideration to the responsibilities of dog ownership? Thousands of people don't. Consequently, our dog welfare societies are full of unwanted dogs. What will you do with your dog at holiday times? Can you afford expensive vet's bills if he's ill? What will you do if you have chosen the wrong puppy and cannot handle him? Over half the dog owners I come into contact with have chosen the wrong dog. In these circumstances, quite a number of things happen. The worst of all is that they dump the dog anywhere, or take it along to the nearest dog shelter. Some of the owners struggle on bravely, constantly battling to be the boss. Consequently, the dog gets more difficult to control and suffers because the owner is unable to take him for long walks. The dog either drags too much on the lead or won't come back when he's allowed his freedom. In extreme cases, an untrained dog will assert his authority completely over his human owner, growling and even biting. Except in some very rare cases, where a dog is mentally unstable, the owner must take the full blame.

What do you do if you already own the wrong dog or have an older dog who is completely untrained? Start at the very beginning, learning first and foremost how to play with your dog. You'll be amazed at the way your relationship changes. Your dog will begin to view you in a different light. He'll be keen to be with you and please you and your training lessons will be a pleasure.

CHAPTER 2

BRINGING PUPPY HOME

Before your new puppy arrives, you must ensure that the home and family are well prepared. If you have children, now is a good time to make various rules and regulations. Children love responsibility, but just like young puppies they do tend to get carried away and an over-enthusiastic young child could so easily ruin your puppy. In my experience, you will gain the best results if you include the children in the responsibility of looking after the puppy. An older child, for example, can be elected to ensure that young children do not constantly pick puppy up. He is not a toy to be played with. Another child could be made responsible for ensuring that a bowl of fresh water is always near the puppy's bed. If shown correctly how to handle and play with a puppy, children and dogs can be the very best of friends. Explain to your children that it's far better for them to sit on the floor and throw a toy or play tug-of-war with the puppy than chase him round and pick him up. One hard and fast rule that must never be broken is that puppy must not be disturbed in his bed. The bed should be regarded as his sanctuary. There can be nothing worse than a tired puppy annoyed by over-enthusiastic children wishing to play, and you could hardly blame a puppy for being annoyed.

Your garden

Have you given a thought to your garden? A young puppy can destroy a beautifully laid out garden in no time at all. If there are parts of your garden you don't wish puppy to go on, they must be fenced off. You can't expect him to understand that the lawn and bean patch are out-of-bounds. Choose an area where you want your puppy to relieve himself. If you always take him to that spot, he'll soon learn.

Final Checklist

The Puppy's Bed: Buy a hard plastic bed for your puppy. I have tried all types on my own dogs. When Bracken came to us at the age of six weeks, I bought a large and rather expensive basket. I never thought for one moment that a tiny, six-week-old puppy could destroy such a large bed, but Bracken proved me wrong. Within fourteen days he had chewed the whole thing. I then provided him with a comfortable, soft foam, bed. This didn't take him as long to destroy as the basket. Within one night he'd shredded it into one inch square pieces of foam. Then I discovered the hard plastic dog beds which are still in my dog room, unchewed.

Try to find an out-of-the-way, secluded, draught-free, spot for your puppy's bed. The most sensible place is the kitchen, or utility room if you have one, where floors are uncarpeted and easily washed. And do remember that puppies are full of mischief and keen to explore. Any cables and plugs should be well out of puppy-teeth range. Vegetable racks and rubbish bins are a positive lure to a young puppy. Puppy's sleeping room should be completely cleared of any chewables, except his own toys. You will need a good supply of doggy blankets. These must be washed very regularly, or your puppy will begin to smell.

Toys: Collect a store of chewable things for the puppy. There is no need to spend a lot of money at the local pet shop on rubber bones and squeaky toys—you have plenty of fascinating chewables in your home. Washing-up liquid containers with the top taken off and well washed out will give your puppy hours of amusement; old socks and tights knotted up; the cardboard tubes from kitchen towels and toilet rolls can be shredded by a young puppy with safety. Put all these things in an old washing-up bowl that you can give to puppy when you want him to amuse himself.

Bowls: It is a sensible idea to write out a list of your puppy's needs before visiting the local pet shop. Beds and bedding; bowls—your puppy will need two: a heavy pot bowl for water and an aluminium bowl for his food. These are completely unchewable and very easy to keep clean. I have discovered that plastic bowls do tend to get scratched or chewed very easily. Buy the heaviest pot bowl you can find for puppy's water. This will prevent him from knocking it around, although Katy, one of my puppies, was fascinated by her large pot water bowl and, from the age of eleven weeks, would carry it, water and all, about the house and garden, leaving a tell-tale trickle of water wherever she went. For a long time I was mystified when I found the water bowl under a chair in the lounge or down the garden on the lawn. I never imagined it was Katy. She was so small that I thought it would be impossible for her to lift such a heavy bowl. I began to believe we had

gremlins in the home, until one day I actually saw her carrying it. I never stopped this little trick of hers. She enjoyed it so much, and it is a Labrador's instinct to carry things around, even if it be a large pot bowl full of water.

Brushes and Combs: If you have a long-coated dog, you'll need a metal comb and a brush. I have found the human plastic bristle brushes are far better for long-coated dogs than the ones sold for the purpose. A smooth-coated dog will need a rubber brush. This fetches out the loose fur far easier and quicker than a bristle brush and an old pair of tights or silk scarf rubbed along a smooth-coated dog will leave the coat gleaming.

You will need a collar and lead even before your puppy gets to the age when he can go into the outside world. A soft leather collar is a must for a small puppy. If you have a toy breed, a cat collar will be ideal.

Be certain that the day of your puppy's arrival is completely clear of other commitments. The worst thing you could do is to bring a new puppy home and then find you have to leave him alone for two or three hours. When I have a new puppy arriving, there's a blitz on the housework the day before so that I can spend every available moment with him. An old hot water bottle is always a useful asset. For the first few nights your puppy will be alone, deprived of canine company. The warmth of a hot-water bottle under his blanket could be just what he needs to send him off into a peaceful sleep. And, on the subject of sleep, try to get plenty before your puppy arrives. The next two weeks could see you haggard and worn dealing with a night howler.

The first day

It is very important for you to understand your puppy, as he does not understand you. Pretend he is a foreigner, and can't understand a word of English. Put yourself in his place for a moment. You're a child and someone has left you in a foreign country. You don't understand a word they're saying to you. The only way you'll learn is by demonstration and constant repetition of the foreign words. This is how your puppy feels in a strange house. No mother or brothers and sisters to run back to for comfort and reassurance. So you must be all things to him—provider, friend, companion, teacher and playmate. With these thoughts in mind, you can begin the first lessons.

House-training

House-training should prove no problem if you're quick and alert to your puppy's needs. He will need to pay frequent visits to his spot in the

31

Show your children the correct way
to play with a puppy

garden: after each meal, after a sleep and any time you think about it in between. Always pick him up and carry him to the spot. Give him a command. I use the words 'busy dog'. Don't dump him and retreat back to the house and close the door. He hasn't a clue what he's been put in the garden for. You must stay with him, repeating your commands over and over again. Whether it's hailing, blowing a gale or a snowstorm's on, you must persevere. As soon as he's been a 'busy dog', give him lots of praise, tell him how clever he is, pick him up and return him to the house. If you are diligent and watch your puppy closely, you will know when he needs to go out. A sure sign will be when he puts his nose to the ground, his tail up in the air and runs round in circles. That is your cue to move speedily with him into the garden.

There is bound to be the odd mistake, but it will be your fault. I can guarantee that your puppy will choose the most inconvenient moment to be a 'busy dog'—when the phone rings, or someone's knocking at the front door. On occasions like these, I don't leave my puppy in the kitchen to get on with it. I pick him up and carry him with me to the door or the phone to ensure that no little accidents happen. When you catch your puppy in the act, tell him 'No', pick him up immediately and rush him to his spot in the garden. If you find a puddle behind the kitchen door, there is no point in reprimanding him, he's forgotten about it. The worst possible thing you can do is to take him and rub his nose in it and then throw him outside. This will give your puppy a complex about relieving himself anywhere and he will try and hide from you. You may then find he's going to relieve himself under beds and behind settees, because he's afraid of you. It's advisable to line the floor with newspapers at night when puppy is to be left alone. You can't expect a six-week-old puppy to go through the night without relieving himself. You wouldn't expect a six-week-old baby to—although one of the blessings of having a puppy is that he's house-trained much quicker than a baby. Puppies are very much like babies—you can't take your eyes off them for a minute without their getting up to some mischief or other, and it is far easier if the whole family are prepared to accept their share of puppy-minding. It's so easy to sit down in the evening after a hard day, and become engrossed in the television, forgetting all about puppy.

Don and I did this one evening when Katy was a few weeks old, although, before settling down to watch the film, I had taken her into the garden so that she could be a 'busy dog'. The other four dogs were curled up in their respective places, and I fully intended to keep an eye on Katy, but the film was far too thrilling. I remember at one point looking round and seeing her tail and back legs sticking out from under the coffee table. Good, I thought, she's fast asleep. I turned my attention back to the screen. Part of my mind must have heard the gentle lapping, and I did notice, once or twice, that Don picked his tankard of beer, looked into it, hummed to himself and went to the pantry where he keeps his supplies. Just after 'The End' appeared on the television screen there was a soft thud. Katy had been asleep on the settee for a time, and the thud was her falling off on to the carpet. She sat up with a puzzled expression on her face and hiccoughed. Don looked across at her, and commented that she was rather bleary-eyed. On closer inspection it was apparent that she was drunk.

'Thank goodness for that,' Don said with a sigh. 'I thought I was going mad. I was sure I filled my tankard up and every time I looked it was empty.'

Katy had been quietly sipping Don's beer. We both laughed until tears ran down our faces to see Katy staggering around the garden that night. But I certainly don't advocate that your puppy has a nightly 'tipple', so watch him carefully.

At around twelve weeks, you can expect your puppy to go through the night. Try him without the newspapers. If there are accidents on the kitchen floor, put the newspapers down again for another few nights. Don't come down in the morning and reprimand your puppy for making a mistake in the night. He does not remember. He thinks you're telling him off for welcoming you as you come through the door. That is not a very good basis for your future relationship.

If your puppy refuses to be clean in the daytime, ask yourself why. Is there something wrong with him? If you suspect this, you must take him to the vet immediately. But, more likely, there is something wrong with your training. If you have bought an older dog who needs house-training, then you have a bigger problem on your hands, in more ways than one. A dog will not usually foul his own bedding area so, if you can, restrict the dog at night when you have to leave him and you should find he gradually becomes clean. In the daytime you should have no problem. By making frequent trips to the garden you will never give him the opportunity to foul the house.

One of the puppies I sold came back to me because it could not be house-trained. I always try to ensure that anyone wanting one of my puppies is offering the right type of home, but in this instance I made a mistake. Fortunately, my puppies only leave here on the understanding that if anything goes wrong they come back and within half an hour of this puppy's return I realised that there was something very wrong with him. Although he was trotting into the garden and being a 'busy dog' on command, he was still dribbling when he returned to the house. I took him to the vet immediately and discovered that he had very bad cystitis, and that this had obviously been going on over the last month or so. Once the family who had originally bought the puppy from me realised this, they wanted him back. Needless to say, I flatly refused, and gave them their money back. If they couldn't spot a case of cystitis that was so obvious in such a young puppy, they weren't responsible owners in my opinion.

Often a puppy, or even an older dog, will be unclean at night because

he is afraid of being alone. In all such cases that I have come into contact with, the puppy has been clean as soon as the owner has let him sleep in their bedroom. I don't advocate that you should have your puppy in your bedroom with you—puppies can be a nuisance at three o'clock in the morning—but it's worth keeping this in mind in case you are unlucky enough to own a dog who gets lonely in the dark. Too much feeding at the wrong time can often cause your dog to foul the kitchen during the night. It is worth experimenting with different types of food, or different times of feeding your dog. It will be obvious if you are feeding too much—he will soon be very fat.

The first night

The first night with your puppy could be a traumatic experience for both of you. You may decide that you wish your puppy to sleep in your bedroom. Fine, but I might warn you it's not a very pleasant experience to be jumped on and bitten in the middle of a peaceful sleep, apart from the fact that your bedroom carpet will not benefit from puppy's puddles. The more acceptable place for a young puppy is in the kitchen. Your bedtime must now become a well thought out, planned affair. For at least half an hour before you wish to retire, play with your puppy. This will, hopefully, tire him out—at least for an hour or so. His supper eaten, you must visit the garden with him and ensure he's a 'busy dog'. Now tell him it's bedtime. Place him in his bed, where his warm hot water bottle is tucked safely in blankets, and put his toy box on the floor so that he can at least amuse himself while you're not there. And now to bed yourself, where you will no doubt lie awake waiting for the first howls. Your attitude on this first major lesson of night howling is very important. A mistake on your part could cause endless sleepless nights.

At the first sound of a squeak run downstairs, being very careful not to stub your toe on the hall table—that will put you in completely the wrong frame of mind to deal with your puppy. Enter the kitchen with confidence and determination. Do not, I repeat, *not* pick your puppy up and make a fuss of him. You are making a rod for your own back. Think of it: if you were he and every time you howled someone came to make a fuss of you, what would you do? You'd howl all the more, of course. Pick your puppy up firmly and place him in his bed, telling him that you will not stand for this noise and it is bedtime. Resist the temptation to be rough with him, however bad-tempered you feel at having your night's sleep disturbed. After all, he is alone, there's no one to comfort him and he doesn't understand this strange house or its ways as yet.

After placing puppy in his bed, retreat in a no-nonsense manner and

A fluffy puppy looks very appealing but can you cope with the heavy coat of an adult dog?

close the door firmly behind you. It's worth standing in the hall for a while, rather than leaping up and down stairs all night, to see if puppy begins to howl again. If he does, you're on the spot to repeat your earlier performance. If the howling becomes really atrocious and you're walking about like a zombie, a gentle shake by the scruff of the neck will not come amiss. I can assure you, it's worth giving up one night's sleep to teach puppy this lesson of night silence. If you ignore the howling now, or give in to him and make a fuss when you enter the kitchen, you will suffer the sounds of your dog for many nights to come. The only dog I ever had night problems with was Buttons. But we had bought her not as a puppy but as an adult dog of a year old. Emma, of course, came up to bed with us and Buttons was put in the kitchen for the night. Quite understandably Buttons did not like this at all. Why should the other dog come to bed while she was relegated to the kitchen? She complained bitterly by barking. There was no way Emma's special place could be intruded upon by another dog and I was determined that Buttons would not bark all night. I honestly can't remember how many times I travelled up and down stairs but I do know it took me from twelve o'clock at night until 5 a.m. in the morning to convince Buttons that no amount of barking was going to give her the pass to our bedroom. Although the first night for me was a sleepless one, it paid off, for Buttons never barked again at night.

Feeding

Food will be one of your puppy's main interests in life. Have you remembered to check with the breeder what your puppy has been fed on? A new house and a different type of food can easily upset a young puppy. A six-week-old puppy should be provided with five meals a day. If your puppy has come from a reliable and conscientious breeder you will have been supplied with a diet sheet with the type of food and quantities he will require, although a few useful hints may help you. I have often found diet sheets from breeders contained too milky or sloppy feeds for a puppy. This can often give diarrhoea. If you have this problem, replace milky or sloppy feeds with meat meals.

One of the biggest mistakes I made when feeding my dogs was to vary their meals. I felt convinced that they would hate to be presented with exactly the same food every day. This was ignorance on my part. Not only did I cause stomach upsets, but I was training my dogs to be choosy. A dog's digestive system is very different from ours and copes best with the same type of meal given at the same time in the day. I do always allow a puppy one dislike, but if he refuses my second offering I remove the bowl until the next meal. A six-week-old puppy should be keen and eager at mealtimes and if he refuses two or three meals in the day then contact your local veterinary surgeon for further advice.

Chewing

The first few days with your puppy will be rather hectic ones. As you are learning to understand each other you will become aware of your puppy's need to chew, and he's bound to chew at things that you don't want him to. When you're chastising your puppy, remember to assess the type of dog he is. For a sensitive dog, just a 'No' in a firm voice—definitely not shouted—will be enough. For a harder, more dominant dog, you may have to take physical action. The very best way of reproof to a puppy is that which their mother uses in the litter—take hold of them by the scruff of the neck and give it a shake, using your disapproving words. You can't hurt your puppy in this manner. Smacking and shouting will make a dog hard and unresponsive towards you. A shake by the loose skin on the back of his neck will make him feel humiliated. Don't leave it at that. If you've stopped him chewing your table leg, you must offer him something else to do. Just stopping a puppy from doing something bad is not enough. Within a few seconds he'll have forgotten all about it and probably the moment you turn your back he'll turn back to the table leg, so give him something else to chew—ideally one of his own toys. Play with him for a minute or two to gain his interest in this new toy, but do remember, puppies are like children and they tend to be wildly enthusiastic about something for a minute or two and then lose complete interest and search for something else to do.

Learn to play

The sure way to own a happy, obedient dog is to play with him as another dog would. If you took great interest in watching the litter play together, then you saw how rough the puppies were, biting each other, rolling over, pulling ears and tails, and the mock fights, the little barks and growls. Now is your great opportunity to become an actor. You must play the part of another puppy, simulating this type of game. Get on the floor, down to his level and, armed with a plaything, you can begin your games. An old pair of tights or knotted sock, anything will do as long as it's shared only at your times of play. The more you can act like another puppy, the more he will love you and respect you. Have mock fights with him and tugs-of-war with his toy and if you can bark and growl at him, all the better. Play throwing your toy but join in the game, try to get it before he can. The more hand contact you have with your puppy the better. Gently roll him over. Use your finger and thumb to give mock bites, as his litter brothers and sisters would do. Don't hurt him by pinching him. This is, after all, a game. If you think I'm talking total lunacy, well, I can only say that you will never gain the mutual respect and understanding it takes to have a happy, obedient companion. For in these moments of play you'll be teaching him all the many different commands.

CHAPTER 3

FIRST LESSONS

Sit

The first lesson you wish your puppy to learn is Sit. When you're in possession of his toy, push your puppy gently down into the Sit position. With your right hand cupped around the puppy's chest, place your left hand on his back near the tail. With your right hand, push gently backwards, while you are easing down with your left. Give a firm, but not loud, command. Never shout at your puppy. It will only lead him to flatten his ears against the noise and ignore you. It's much better to talk quietly, then he has to make the effort of listening to you. As soon as his bottom is on the floor in the correct position, throw his toy. Repeat this over and over again in your games, which can take place as often and for as long as puppy is keen to play. He'll have a marvellous time with you. As far as puppy is concerned, he's not learning anything, for the Sit position is part of the fun.

Down

The Down should be taught at your playtimes just like the Sits. Once puppy is interested in the toy get him to chase it along the floor, so that his head is down looking at his toy, then with your left hand use a slight pressure on his shoulders, gently down and sideways to take him off balance into the Down position. Once puppy is down let him have his toy. Give him lots of praise. I have often seen trainers take hold of a front leg or even two front legs to get puppy into a Down. This must be very frightening and can also be dangerous. Remember only to practise your Downs on a soft floor or a carpet, never on tiled floors or concrete. Give a gentle, but firm 'Down' command each time and don't forget your rapturous praise and lots of play with his toy. It is ineffective to teach a puppy to go into the Down position from the Sit as many trainers do. You will not get such a fast response on your command of 'Down' in the future. If you can teach puppy how to go down on the move, or from a stand position, he will be a lot more inclined to obey you with speed.

Puppy come

Your games can also include the command Come, the most important command you'll ever teach your dog. Each time he's coming towards you, give his name and say 'Come'. This will instill the word into his mind and it will be associated with fun and pleasure. Use your puppy's name as often as you can, except if you're telling him off. Never, ever use his name to reprimand him. This is most important in his first few weeks with you. His name should be associated with coming to you for pleasure. You will find a young puppy is either fast asleep or tearing about the place with great enthusiasm. You must channel this enthusiasm from an early age, either by playing as I've explained and teaching him commands, or giving him something to do. To him the world is new and exciting. He wants to see everything, taste everything and smell everything, all in one go. Every minute of his waking life is an adventure. If you can share it with him and put him on the right lines, you'll have a marvellous relationship.

I do know from past experience that it is impossible to watch puppy every minute of the day, so when things happen just remember that puppy is bored and he needs to be on the go all the time. Personally, I cannot just sit. If I'm sitting down I must watch television, or knit or read. I would go mad if I just had to sit, and this is how a puppy is. You can't expect him to sit and be quiet for long periods. I can remember only too well what my puppies have done in those moments when I have forgotten to keep my eye on them. Bracken, who was an exceptionally quiet and well-behaved puppy, always lulled me into a false sense of security that he was behaving himself perfectly and I could go off and do the housework without worrying. On one occasion, when I was far too engrossed in cleaning out the bathroom to check on Bracken's antics, he chewed through the phone wire and a cable on the standard lamp. Another time, when I was convinced that he was playing quietly and happily in the garden and that there was no need to keep checking on his whereabouts, he was having a wonderful time pulling every rose tree out of the ground and chewing the roots. If these things happen to you, do remember why puppy does them, and when chastising him, keep his temperament in mind. Katy, in one of my moments of inattention, crept into the lounge and spied a vase full of chrysanthemums. They were obviously a great temptation, and she chewed all the flowers and shredded the petals—I would never have imagined chrysanthemums could go so far. The lounge carpet, which is normally red and gold, was changed into purples, white and yellows. I must admit that on seeing the chaos my first instinct was to laugh, for Katy was still covered in chrysanthemum petals. But puppies aren't stupid. If you show amusement at their naughty antics, they will remember and do it to amuse you in the future. Instead, I put my stern voice on and said, 'Katy, you wicked puppy, you shouldn't

Young puppies should be carried out to accustom them to the outside world

have done that!' Instantly, her expression changed from total glee to actual terror and she fled and hid under the armchair. In this case, my tone had obviously been too severe for such a sensitive puppy.

If I'm giving you the impression that a puppy is a twenty-four hour a day job then you're right. Whenever I have a new puppy in the home, I'm totally exhausted. I do my housework and other jobs while puppy is asleep so that I can give my full attention to him in his waking hours. It's hard work for the first few months but it's well worth it for the pleasure of future years that I'll share with my well-behaved dogs.

Socialisation

Part of the secret of having a well-trained puppy is the ability on your part to think ahead. You won't be able to take him for a walk outside until he's completed his injections, at about fourteen to sixteen weeks. This is far too late to introduce your puppy to a collar and lead and the outside world. The socialisation of your puppy at an early age is essential if you require a well-adjusted adult dog. I discovered this, to my cost, with Bracken, my first puppy. I never thought of taking him out on to the streets until he was sixteen weeks old. At home, he was perfectly behaved and afraid of nothing and walked well in the garden on a collar and lead. You can imagine my surprise at our first day's outing. The moment we stepped out of the gate, Bracken flattened himself to the pavement with terror at the sound and sights of traffic. Luckily for me, Labradors are normally bold and friendly by nature, and just a little thought on my part put the whole thing right. I took him to the gate every day, sat on the ground to reassure him and within a few days he'd gained enough confidence to walk on the lead. But even to this day, at the age of five, he can still be a little wary of strange objects he sees on the pavement. But that taught me a lesson I shall never forget and it has never happened with any of the other dogs I have owned.

Carry your puppy out with you as early as possible, for a walk round the block, to the local shops, anywhere as long as your puppy can see and hear traffic. Encourage people to come and stroke him. It's in the first two or three months of a puppy's life that fear of traffic or strangers can build up. The more varied the situations you can introduce the puppy to, the better. Let him watch milk vans, dustbin lorries and roadworks if you have them in your area. Do remember to talk to your puppy. Tell him there's nothing to be afraid of. You might feel rather stupid explaining what a dustbin lorry is to a puppy but you'll be amazed how many words your puppy will learn. My dogs often give a bark or two at the sound of the milkman approaching, until I tell them it's only the milkman. Then they quieten down and get back on their beds. You have, I am sure, heard many dog owners say, 'He understands every word, you know.' I am positive that dogs understand far more words than we give them credit for.

The other night, I tried an experiment to prove beyond doubt that my dogs do understand words that we haven't actually taught them. Before bedtime all our dogs go out into the garden and Buttons is always the last in. I know what she is doing out there, she is hoping to find food. I am afraid Buttons lives to eat and she will not come into the kitchen until she has investigated every inch of the garden and is sure no morsel of food is left out there. She will even sit sometimes with her nose pointing towards the sky, as if it will suddenly rain doughnuts or dog biscuits! So, when she didn't appear with all the other dogs, I decided to trick her. I stood at the kitchen door and shouted 'Don't snatch!', which are the words I use when I am offering our dogs their biscuits. It means exactly what it says, because Labradors are notorious for grabbing half your hand as well as the biscuit offered. At once I heard Buttons galloping down the garden. She rushed into the kitchen and looked at me expectantly, then she looked at all the other dogs, sniffed around and sat in front of me with a look of disbelief on her face. I had shouted 'Don't snatch'; that meant food being handed out; so *where* was it?

It would be quite a worthwhile project to write down each week the new words your puppy has learnt, such as dinnertime, or bedtime, or sit and come. As your list grows, so will your respect for your dog and understanding of his canine intelligence.

Lead training

While you are showing your puppy the outside world by carrying him about with you, you can be lead training him in the garden. Choose a soft, lightweight leather collar for this purpose. It must be quite humiliating to have something thrust around your neck and to find that, whatever you do, you can't free yourself. So it's up to you to make your puppy associate the collar and lead with pleasure. You can start putting the collar on your puppy at quite a young age, seven to eight weeks. Do this before your play, then your puppy won't have time to think of his collar, he'll be too interested in his toy and your games together.

Your first lesson of lead training in the garden is the most important. It's amazing how puppy can remember your mistakes. Choose a time when you are in an exceptionally good mood, so that you can keep the whole thing light and cheerful. Don't do it on the day you've received a gas bill. I am still amazed at the perception of my dogs to my innermost feelings, and if I feel the slightest bit bad tempered or under the weather, they know. To be perfectly honest with you, my dogs have made me a far better person. I've had to become good-natured both outside and in, far more active and much more patient. I often need to cajole myself into the right frame of

The Recall
TOP Always get down to puppy's level
when teaching the Recall
BOTTOM Remember to reward puppy with
a titbit and praise when he comes to you

mind before doing any lessons with the dogs by first of all having a game with them, just rolling about on the floor, enjoying myself as much as the dog enjoys himself.

So, when you've had a good roll on the lawn with the dog and dusted yourself down, now is the time to begin your lead training, armed with puppy's favourite toy. Depending on the temperament of your puppy, he will have different reactions to the lead—from sitting and refusing to budge an inch, to trying to drag you round the garden. We'll deal with the 'I'm not budging an inch' puppy first of all. Just put yourself in his place for a moment: there you are with something round your neck and a lead attaching you to a human being—not a very pleasant thought. So it's up to you to make it a fun time. Throw the toy in front of your puppy. If he still shows no inclination to move you retrieve the toy and continue doing so. I haven't come across many puppies who can resist this temptation. If your puppy is one of them, then I'm afraid he views you as a dead loss and you must try to relax, let your hair down, have fun. Don't just stand there like a dried-out lettuce leaf. Do something!

Once you have puppy moving on the lead, give him a command. I use the word Steady. It's a calming word, unlike Sit and Down, which are quite sharp and should be sharply carried out. You need a calm, relaxed dog on the other end of the lead, so give the command in a calm, reassuring manner. Once your puppy has confidence walking beside you on the lead, you can dispense with the toy. But don't dispense with your voice. The lead is a physical connection with your dog, the voice is the mental one.

If your puppy tries to drag you round the garden, take action now. It may be quite amusing to see a small, eight-week puppy tugging on the other end of the lead, but it won't be very amusing when he's a huge brute of an animal dragging you along the streets. Never let bad habits begin and you'll have no problems. A small puppy is very easy to handle and doesn't need jerking or yanking. When he pulls, give a small, playful tug with your command Steady. Try to develop a feeling for your lead. It's no good letting your puppy throw his weight into the collar. This has a similar effect to putting a horse in front of a cart in a harness. He throws all of his weight into the harness to pull the cart and so your dog throws his weight into the collar to pull you. He is only able to do that if the lead is tight. As soon as you feel the slightest tension on the lead, give your little tug. You must judge the length of your lead yourself. Too much and he'll be leaping around your legs and tying you in knots. Too little and he'll be strung up by the neck. It doesn't matter which side you walk your puppy on, although the accepted side is on the left, but once you've chosen, stick to it. To keep swopping puppy from side to side is very confusing for him.

Keep your lead training lessons short and interesting. Always play before and afterwards and remember, you're teaching your puppy a new

English word. It will take time and patience.

A word about the collar

I am very worried about the current enthusiasm for check-chain collars. The public seem to believe the be-all and end-all of training their dog is having it on the end of a chain. I agree there is a time and place for a check-chain collar, but it is certainly not on a puppy under six months of age, and, in my opinion, should not be used by inexperienced people. If you train your puppy correctly from the beginning, there will never be any need to revert to a chain. Seventy-five per cent of dog owners have a dragging dog. Why? Because they didn't think to train their dog at an early age. I have seen four- and five-month-old puppies completely out of hand and then it's so easy and so much less trouble to put a chain around the dog's neck, whereas a little effort and patience on the owner's part would prevent this. It's worth remembering that the more you let your dog pull, the more he will develop his neck muscles, until eventually he will be so strong that even a check-chain collar will not prevent him from dragging you down the road. I prefer to use a half check-chain on the older dog that has got out of hand. It cannot be put on wrongly and, used with the right technique, can be as effective as a full check-chain without any of the disastrous results. Most owners blame their dogs for pulling. I get many desperate dog owners confiding in me: 'Of course, it's his own fault,' they tell me. 'Look at him, he's choking himself on the end of that chain.' These poor dogs have never had the opportunity of the correct training. They always believe the chain around their neck will be tight and so constantly try to get away from it. If you've ever used a chain lead and had it wrapped around your hand with a pulling dog, you will soon feel the effect it has on your flesh. So why do such a vast amount of owners not think it has any effect on the flesh of a dog's neck? It all boils down to mutual respect and unless you have respect for your dog, he will never have any respect for you.

The Recall

The garden is a very good place for training your puppy to come back to you. If he won't come back in the garden, he's not going to come back when you let him off the lead in the fields. When you see that your puppy is engrossed in some exciting new smell, call him. Now is the time to put your extrovert character into use. Your calls should be of great excitement. Pretend you've just won £250,000 on the pools and you are telling the world about it. There aren't many puppies who can resist that sort of call. Most of them will come galloping back to see what all the excitement is about. At which time, you sit on the ground and either give him a titbit or play with his favourite toy. If puppy refuses to come to you, try sitting on the ground and playing with his toy, throwing it up and down in the air and using lots of exciting words like Hooray or Yippee. Don't worry about the neighbours, they'll be convinced you've lost your marbles, but who cares?

If your puppy still ignores you, you have a hard nut to crack and I don't envy you. Now is the time to use low, animal cunning. While your puppy is totally engrossed, creep up behind him and give him a gentle little pinch on the back leg, then dash away shouting joyously. As far as puppy's concerned, it wasn't you who touched him but some invisible monster and his automatic reaction will be to come to you for reassurance.

These exercises should be carried out as many times a day as possible, until you get an instant reaction from your puppy. Whenever you call he comes. Dinnertime is always a good reinforcement of the recall, so remember to use the same commands of calling your puppy in when you offer his dinner.

CHAPTER 4

TEACHING YOUR PUPPY THE MEANING OF WORDS

It is important for you to remember that your puppy does not understand English. It is essential to show him exactly what the words mean. Most dog owners don't realise that they have actually taught the puppy to do the wrong thing by not using action and words together. A good example of this is a puppy who tries to climb on the furniture. Just think of it for a moment. You're the puppy, you have two paws on the settee and your owner is sitting reading the paper in an armchair. 'Get off!' your owner will shout. But he can't be bothered to put the paper down, come across to you and physically show you what he means. So, what are you to think, after he's stayed sitting for quite some time, telling you to get off? If you are a reasonably intelligent puppy, as most puppies are, you will associate the words 'Get off' with having your front two paws on the furniture. (And, as you get a little older and bigger, your two back paws will be on the furniture as well.) As your owner is still there, reading his paper, saying 'Get off!', you think to yourself, That's all right. He means I can sit here. The day he gets annoyed about it, decides to use some action and hauls you off the settee, what are you to think? You're confused. You don't trust him any more. You make a decision there and then that your owner is irrational and can often tell you one thing and mean another.

So many misunderstandings are caused simply because the owner does not think. How many times have you seen people shouting at their dogs to get down when the puppies are jumping up and then in the next moment screaming at their dog to sit down? Down should mean *one* thing, lie down. A simple mistake like this can cause your puppy great confusion, even to the extent of being afraid of you because he doesn't understand. Your choice of commands must be very carefully selected so that they all sound completely different. If my dogs jump up I use the word Off. Practice and patience are the by-words of dog training and remember never to give your puppy a command unless you actually show him what you mean. Think for a moment of the amount of time mothers spend with their toddlers. Every single thing is new to a baby and must be explained over and over again. Mothers spend hours taking the toddler round the garden, showing them flowers and birds, grass and trees. Every item of food they are given, they are told exactly what is it. It takes months of constant repetition for a young baby to understand each word and associate it with the right object.

Most people don't remember this learning process as they grow up, but as visual learning came to me as an adult, I have a much clearer understanding of the necessity to show and teach. When I was able to see objects clearly for the first time at twenty-nine, I had to learn by touch and association. My brain was unable to translate visual images to me. They were there all right and I could see them clearly, but I didn't understand what they were. A simple thing like a cup on a table was an enigma to me until I picked up the cup and felt it. It was only then my brain could associate the sense of touch and tell me what the object was. It's a strange but wonderful thing to be able to discover the visual world as an adult and it has given me a much clearer understanding of what it must feel like to be learning everything, not only the visual things in the world but the language and the sounds and the actions.

I can imagine and sympathise with how distracted a young puppy must be with so many new smells and images. A young puppy doesn't have the capability to concentrate on what you're telling him all the time. There are so many other things he wishes to investigate. Therefore, it is up to you to gain your puppy's attention. You are competing with all these new things your puppy is seeing for the first time. As yet, he understands nothing of the human way of life. A new puppy in my home will accompany me everywhere and all the time I keep up a non-stop chatter. 'This is the bathroom.' 'I'll go and make the bed.' 'The phone's ringing.' 'I must go and put the dinner on.' It might sound quite stupid to be telling a young puppy all these things, but they do learn if only they're given the opportunity. And while I'm taking my puppy around the house, I incorporate my training lessons.

Training around the house

I keep a store of worn tights on my dressing table and each time I go to make the bed my new puppy is asked to do something—a Sit or a Down, say—and I throw an old pair of tights and have a little game. An ideal opportunity to teach puppy all the do's and don'ts is while you're going around the house. Katy, my little black Labrador puppy, soon realised the things that she could carry about and the things that were absolutely taboo by this method. Upstairs I would find her ferreting under Kerensa's bed for inviting-looking teddy bears or furry slippers. Being a Labrador, she would come and show me her prize with tail wagging and ears flicking. The first instinct of most pet owners would be to make a grab for the puppy's prize, shout and reprimand them. The puppy, of course, runs off in terror. You haven't taught your puppy not to chew things that aren't his own, all you've done is taught him not to bring them to you. Each time Katy brought me a prize, I took a pair of tights from the dressing table, approached her gently and took the article from her mouth with a very quiet but firm 'No, Katy', and threw her a pair of knotted tights. Consequently, she never chewed anything that wasn't hers. For everything she found she brought to me, knowing I wouldn't rant and rave but would replace her prize with something she could chew and play with to her heart's content.

It is far easier to train your puppy if he is constantly with you around the house than making a set period of time each day for training lessons. This is boring for the dog and the owner. It's much nicer to integrate training into the household duties. For instance, while I'm waiting for the kettle or the potatoes to boil, I've got a minute to teach my puppy the word Wait. I actually have three different commands for what I call the Steady-Sit. Many trainers use one, usually Stay, but as I require a steady sit for three different types of circumstance, I have split them into Wait, Stay and Stop there.

I use the command Wait when I expect a puppy to sit and wait for another command. I use the word Stay for a Sit from puppy and a Stay whatever happens until I return to his side. Stop there, I use when I need to leave my puppy outside a shop. Stop there to my puppy means there's no need to sit perfectly still, you can lie down or stand up, but you must stay in that same place until I return. The three different commands mustn't be taught at once, but as a gradual process. One must be quite clear to your puppy before you proceed to the next command. I prefer to teach Wait first, as I find this the most useful.

The Wait command

With the puppy sitting on your left-hand side, give a quiet, but firm, Wait command. Do not use puppy's name. Puppy should always associate his name with coming to you and we do not wish him to do that on this occasion. Take one small pace to your right, count one second and return to your dog and praise him. He shouldn't have had time to move. If he has, just patiently put him back into the Sit position and try again. You are only expecting puppy to wait there for one second. Extend your puppy's waiting time very gradually. If you rush it, puppy will want to come to you and you have achieved nothing. Many puppies lose their confidence if they think their owner is leaving them. It's not a bad thing that your puppy wants to be with you constantly, so you must build his confidence up. You are not going to be far away, only one pace to start with. Never get annoyed with him for following you. Just be patient and take him back to his original

*The Stop There command
is a must for the busy housewife*

spot. When you can achieve three or four paces away from puppy and a ten second wait, you can then start making use of this new command. For instance, when you open the back door for puppy to go into the garden, ask him to sit and wait while you open the door. This prevents puppies from leaping up at doors in excitement. Then you can tell him, 'Out you go', and make it clear that he's released.

Another excellent use of the Wait command is at the top of the stairs. It's infuriating and very dangerous to have a puppy galloping through your legs as you descend the stairs. Sit puppy at the top of your stairs and command him to wait while you take one or two paces down and then release him by giving him your recall command, Puppy come. Make a lot of fuss of him as you go downstairs together. Extend your steps each day until you can get to the bottom of the stairs and give your recall. It's exciting for a puppy to run downstairs, so it will not only enforce the Wait command while he sits at the top, but it will enforce your recall command as he gallops joyously down the stairs to greet you.

While on the subject of recalls, I must point out a big failing with many trainers. On the recall command, they often ask their puppy to sit in front of them on his return. In my opinion, this is a big put-off to a young puppy. He's come to you with great delight and as soon as he arrives you tell him to sit. What a disappointment to him and an added aggravation to be constantly nagged at to sit when he's reached you. You should never do this. When puppy comes to you, you should make a fuss of him. If you don't like him jumping up you then get down on the floor to his level.

Jumping up

I like my dogs to jump up. It is their way of showing affection and signifies to me a happy dog. In fact, I use this habit from the dogs as a reward. Whenever they've done well, I clap my hands, which is a signal to them to jump up and, as far as my dogs are concerned, it's the richest of praises from me. I admit, there are times when even I don't want the dogs to jump up: when they've come in wet and muddy and I am in my best clothes, just about to leave for a social engagement, for example. No problem. My dogs respond immediately to a command of Off—which means not to jump up—or Sit. But to get this type of response when your dog is excited, you need total control.

Before you make the decision of whether your dog should jump up or not, think about this. What do you do when you meet someone you love very dearly? Throw your arms about them and hug them. That is what your dog is doing, only in his own way. How would you feel if your nearest and dearest pushed you away on greeting, shouting and complaining that you were ruining his suit? I may have convinced you, but what (I can hear you ask) about all the visitors who aren't doggy minded? If your dog is allowed to show his affection towards you, he will be far less inclined to greet strangers in this manner. Make your decision early with your young puppy. Don't wait until he's six months and large and gets into the habit of jumping up. It's far too late to alter his ways then. Even an eight-week-old puppy will jump up. His front paws will probably only reach your ankles. Nevertheless, this is the time to teach him the word Off. Push him down, gently but firmly, saying the word 'Off', put him into the Sit position and then throw his toy. If you repeat this on every occurrence, you will only need to ask your puppy to sit when he's about to jump up. He'll be only too pleased to comply. He knows you are going to produce his toy, throw it and then have a game.

The older puppy or adult dog may take a little more persuading. A good method, with a larger dog who constantly jumps up, is to take hold of his front paws and squeeze until he pulls away. Give him the command Off, put him into the Sit position and treat him as you would a puppy; throw a toy and have a game. There must always be a reward at the end of your lesson. If you purely push the dog off and nag at him, you've taught him nothing except rejection. Another good method with a very large dog whose paws tend to reach to your shoulders, is to push with your feet against his back paws that are on the floor. Push very gently with your toe. It will unbalance him and he will immediately jump down. But don't forget to give your command and reward him.

How to gain total control

Total control is only achieved after much repetition and patience. Never, ever give your puppy a command without actually showing him how to do it. For example, if you ask your puppy to sit, you put him into the Sit position. Don't stand, constantly nagging at him, 'Sit . . . sit . . . sit.' All you're training him to do is ignore you. He must learn from a young age that everything in life contains discipline and fun, no matter what you do together. The more lessons you can think up round the house, the better behaved and more educated puppy you'll have.

Bowl manners

At about the age of ten weeks, you should teach your puppy bowl manners. There's nothing more infuriating than a dog who leaps about at meal times, barking and whining, and who tries to gobble his dinner from the bowl before it's reached the floor. Once your puppy's meal is prepared, put him into the Sit position and hold him by the collar. Place the bowl on the floor and tell him to Leave. Just restrain him from taking his dinner for one second. He is only a puppy and you are teaching him a new English word. Then release him, tell him he is a good boy and he can have his dinner. This can be extended very gradually from, say, one second to maybe twenty seconds when he's six months old.

The command Leave is invaluable, especially if you own Labradors, who, in my experience, are the biggest vacuum cleaners on earth and will eat anything they find in the fields, edible or not. But if your puppy is well versed in the command Leave, it will save him many tummy upsets and a lot of vet's bills.

CHAPTER 5

CAR TRAINING

The worst thing you can possibly do is introduce your puppy to the car on his first journey to the vet for his inoculations. A sensitive puppy will remember this traumatic experience and link the car journey with the vet. Stop problems before they begin and you'll never have any. Don't be tempted to rush any part of your puppy's training. It would be so easy to put puppy in the car and go, and you could be lucky and have a dog who enjoyed car riding. But if the puppy you have has any qualms whatsoever about the car, you may be instilling a fear of the vehicle in him that will take years to cure.

First of all, introduce your puppy to the stationary car. If you have the hatchback variety, you have a ready-made spot in the back for your puppy. Otherwise, a place on the back seat should be allocated to him. Tell puppy exactly what you're doing and use the word 'car' frequently, so that he associates it. Sit him in the place you wish him to regard as his own in the vehicle. Make it interesting for him, with lots of calming words and plenty of praise. He will no doubt be inquisitive and dive over all the seats and investigate every inch. From the very beginning, you must insist that he doesn't leap over the seats: there's nothing more dangerous to a driver than a dog who darts this way and that when the car is in motion. As soon as he attempts to put his front paws over a seat, lift him down gently, tell him No and firmly put him back in his place.

When you feel your puppy is accustomed to the car, you can move on to the next stage, teaching your puppy to wait when the car door is opened. It would be dreadful, on your first journey, to have your puppy dive out of the car on to a main road and be killed. Keep this in mind. It will ensure that you teach your puppy the word Wait correctly when he's in the car. He's obviously had a good grounding in this command but, being in a strange place and different surroundings, you will no doubt need to reinforce this training. Place puppy in the car and close the door. Wait a second or two before re-opening the door, giving your puppy a firm command of Wait. If he makes the slightest attempt to move towards the door, place him back in his spot and repeat your command.

You will also need a command which releases him out of the car—'Good boy, out you come,' for example. Obviously a small puppy cannot make the leap from a car to the ground, so he must wait for you to lift him. Once you've placed puppy on the ground, put him into the Sit position. It's

pointless training him to wait while you open the door, to see him gallop off into the distance once you've given him his command to get out of the car. Puppy must understand that, once out, he sits and waits for you. This doesn't all happen in a day. Do it very carefully and gradually, ensuring that your Wait command in the car is perfect before you begin to teach puppy to sit once he's outside it. Don't forget to give him lots of reassurance and praise.

It would be very unusual, at this point, to find a puppy who really hates the car. This normally happens when the vehicle is in motion and the puppy has not had a chance to accustom himself to this strange new thing. Your next step is to start the engine and let the puppy get used to the sound. If he shows any distress, sit with him a while and comfort him, telling him there's nothing to be afraid of. At this stage, you must watch the reactions of your puppy carefully and keep in mind the type of temperament he has. If he shows fear and whines and shivers, it's reassurance he needs. Giving him his favourite toy to amuse him could help take his mind off the noise of the car. If, on the other hand, he's a dominant type of dog and rushes about barking, now is the time to take positive action by taking hold of him by the scruff of the neck and telling him, in a good firm voice, that that type of behaviour will not be acceptable.

Exactly the same training goes for your first small ride in the car. It would be a great advantage if you could be free to attend to your puppy while someone else drives the vehicle for you. The dominant puppy who barks only needs firm handling. Don't give up. If he jumps out of his place a thousand times, put him back and make him understand that he is not allowed to dive about the vehicle or bark. Here, it is your patience that is needed more than anything else. Give in once to your puppy and you might as well throw in the towel as far as dog training is concerned. You must always win. The puppy who is afraid will take more time and gentler handling to bring round. Something to chew in the car will probably take his mind off his fear. Extreme fear should be dealt with immediately by constantly putting puppy in the car and feeding him a titbit before and after a short journey.

The carsick dog

Carsickness can be a major problem, but in the cases I have dealt with, it has been cured within a week. The car must become associated with pleasure to the carsick dog and the simplest way of achieving this is by taking puppy to a pleasant place—the park or fields—where he can have a free run. If the carsick puppy is not allowed to walk on the lead to his free-run area, but taken each day in the car, it will channel his mind to the pleasure at the end of the journey, not the journey itself. Needless to say, if this type of training fails, you should contact your veterinary surgeon, as

Our dogs waiting for the release command from the car

there are now some very effective tablets available for dogs to prevent travel sickness.

Bed-training

An added aid to car training is to teach your puppy what Bed means. At various times in the day, pick puppy up and take him to his bed, giving him the command 'On your bed'. Stay with him for a moment or two and stroke him, then release him and tell him 'Off you go'. Puppies cannot do anything for very long, they're like babies, so don't insist that puppy stays on his bed for hours on end. Five or six times a day you can pick puppy up and take him to his bed, giving him the command and expecting him to stay just for one or two minutes.

You will soon know when he has a grasp of this new command. All you will need to say is 'On your bed' and he will trot off and lie down for a moment or two. The blanket from his bed can then be put in his elected spot in the car. The words 'On your bed' will then indicate to puppy that you wish him to settle down for a while.

It takes a tremendous amount of patience and effort on your part to teach your puppy anything. But the only sure way of having a well-behaved dog is to take everything in small stages. You wouldn't expect your child to pick up a book and read it, unless he'd first learnt the alphabet. So it is with a young puppy. Only by keeping your training time short and interesting, teaching each command separately—such as Wait and bed-training and Off you go—will you achieve the whole behaviour pattern. A vast majority of the dog-owning public fondly imagine that their puppies will become better behaved as they grow older, without training. I can warn you now that this is not the case and you will not end up with a dog who is a pleasure to be with unless you have the time and patience while he's a young puppy. I have seen so many dogs, at the age of six months, out of control. They won't sit quietly in the car, or respond to the Wait command and do not understand the word Bed. The owners of these dogs firmly believe that six months of age is the correct time to start training their dog. If you follow all my training exercises correctly and thoroughly, by the age of six months your dog will be a paragon of virtue compared to the vast majority of other canines.

HE'S GOT MY BLESSED SLIPPERS NOW...

Don't worry dear, he'll soon grow out of it

BRUCE WAITE

CHAPTER 6

YOUR FIRST WALK

Puppy's first walk into the outside world should be viewed with great importance but, first of all, I would like you to think carefully about your puppy and his feelings. Try to put yourself into his place and understand how he views the outside world. If you have carried him out with you over the past few weeks, there should be no fear in his mind and, ideally, you will have lead and collar trained him in your own back garden as well. Nevertheless, you must accept the fact that, to your puppy, walking out is a new and wonderful experience. He will look upon the pavements as a kaleidoscope of smells. Every blade of grass, gate-post and telegraph pole will be an exciting experience for him. Even if you have managed to make yourself the centre of your puppy's life, you will still be taking a back seat as far as he is concerned. He will dash from this place to that with great exuberance, apparently ignoring your every command. Now is the time for you to show understanding. Think of it this way. Imagine you're taking a six-year-old child to Disneyland. You wouldn't nag and scream at the child for showing delight and enthusiasm on the sights and sounds he experiences. You would try to share it with him, while at the same time keeping control, not letting him run about or make a nuisance of himself. This is how you should approach your puppy's first walk.

Armed with your puppy's favourite toy and some tasty titbits, you can embark on your first outing. You must have an attitude of quiet determination not to let puppy drag you this way and that, or bark at strange sights, or get caught up with his lead. Walk purposefully along the pavement, giving the puppy the same command you've been using in the garden, with lots of encouragement. Stopping to let him have a little sniff here and there is quite acceptable at this point. After all, we do want the puppy to enjoy his first walk. Diving in front of your legs to get to a gate-post should be taboo. If puppy dives in front of you, put your left foot up to stop him. *I do not mean kick your puppy.* A young puppy, especially the toy breeds, should be made aware of your feet. They can be very dangerous to him and he can be very dangerous to you by diving in front of you. Give him a calm, but firm, Steady command and walk on, with plenty of encouragement. If puppy tries to stop and sit on the pavement, give your friendly little tugs, with plenty of excitement in your voice. Don't forget, you have the titbits in your pocket to encourage him along and the toy to stop and play with him occasionally. This is a big new world he's found and while sharing the experience with

*Do not be afraid to
stop and play with your
puppy in the street*

him, you must also remind him constantly that you are there and the best method is to stop and play or give a titbit along the way.

If puppy tries to drag you along, throwing his weight into the collar constantly, be patient. Bring him back with those little tugs and don't forget your command each time. Actions are pointless without words. A well-mannered puppy should sit at kerbs. It prevents him diving into the gutter and adds a little more discipline to his daily life. Sit him at the kerb, just for a second or two, giving him lots of praise and stroking him calmly, then give him the command Steady as you cross the road. You'll be amazed how quickly puppy will automatically sit on reaching a kerb.

Meeting other dogs

If you meet another dog on your first walk, be careful. Think about the long-lasting effect your actions could now have on puppy. If you scoop him up into your arms, showing fear that the other dog may come along and gobble him up, your puppy may be afraid of other dogs for the rest of his life and, depending on his temperament, this could be shown in extreme fear or could turn to positive viciousness. A young puppy should be encouraged to socialise with his canine friends but in a controlled situation. If you were a human being living alone, wouldn't you feel the need to communicate with beings of your own kind? Well, that's just how your puppy feels. But you must not encourage bad behaviour by letting him bark and drag you to other dogs. If your puppy behaves like this at the sight of another dog, stop, put him into a Sit and give him the command to Wait. If he persists with his barking, take hold of the loose skin on the scruff of his neck, gently shake it with a firm command of No. If you do not win at this stage in your puppy's education, you will end up with a total lunatic. If you know the approaching dog to be friendly, do let your puppy have a chat with him. As soon as he is near enough, give your puppy a command which means release, Off you go, or Say hello then. Give puppy a minute or two to socialise with his friend before continuing on your walk. Prising your puppy away from his canine mate may cause you some problems. Now you must assert your authority. You must mix pleasant encouragement with dogged determination. Your puppy must learn that although he is allowed to mix with other dogs, you and you alone give the orders. Give your puppy his walk command, Steady puppy, and a friendly little tug on the lead. He will, no doubt, completely ignore you. Another little tug, with a firmer Steady command and then lots of encouragement. Bring a toy or titbit from your pocket to try to lure him away. If he takes no notice of you, make lots of fuss and enthusiastic noises and carry on with your walk. My enthusiastic noises are usually Yippee and Hooray. I am sure you will cringe inside at the thought of walking along the pavement shouting words like this. The trouble with we British is that we're far too conservative and hate to show our feelings, especially to a dog out in the street. You must forget your inhibitions if you want a well-trained and happy dog. A really good dog trainer would probably win an Oscar for the best acting. I have never had inhibitions about talking to my dogs because of Emma. I needed to talk to her all the time we were working together in order to keep our sealed unit. Being blind, I never saw other people or their reactions to my constant chatter and now it comes second nature to me and I probably do some very foolish things in the street. You'll often see me sitting at a kerb with a new puppy to encourage him to sit steady and reassure him about traffic. You might even see me barking at an approaching dog. I discovered this method of communication while I was working with Emma. Stray and unwanted dogs would often follow us on our way to work and, however much I shouted and threatened, they would not leave us alone, until I decided to try a bark. Dogs are astounded at a human being barking, and so shocked that they invariably turn tail and run.

Back to your puppy's encounter. If none of these encouragements will prise him away from his new found friend, you must now turn to single-minded determination. Take hold of puppy by the scruff of the neck and give him a very firm command of Leave! and then insist that he follows you along the pavement.

If you have chosen one of the more sensitive puppies, the 3s and 4s, you may find your problem of dog encounters in reverse. Your puppy could show extreme fear at the approach of a strange dog. Take your time now and be very patient, for after a few more weeks this could be irrevocable. First of all get down to your puppy's level and put him into the Sit and Wait position. Reassure him with plenty of hand contact and calming words. As the strange dog approaches, ensure your puppy stops in his Wait position, regardless of his whines and squeaks of terror. Approach this situation as you would a child frightened of thunder. Too much sympathy and the child will play on it, and so will your puppy. Calm reassurance is by far the best method, telling the puppy he is very silly to be afraid of another dog. Assuming you know the approaching dog is friendly and fully under control, insist that your puppy sits quietly and encourage him to meet the other dog. Talk to the other dog and stroke it and show your puppy you are quite unafraid. Be patient. In time your puppy is bound to come round. Curiosity is bound to get the better of him and he will want to sniff the strange dog. Any fear shown by your puppy on his first few walks, such as strange dogs, motorbikes, even people, should be approached in a similar manner: stopping, reassuring puppy and not allowing him to be afraid. If you have built up a rapport with your puppy at home and in the garden at playtimes, you can use these techniques even out on the pavement so that puppy forgets his fears of strange sights and sounds and becomes more aware of you.

Let your puppy socialise with other dog

YOUR FIRST WALK

The bolder puppy thinks the whole world is his friend and wants to leap up at every stranger. He must be kept in control now. It is funny to see a tiny puppy trying to climb up the legs of a stranger, but it won't be in the least bit amusing when it's raining or your dog has grown to the size of a Great Dane. If your puppy is inclined to leap up at the nearest human being, stop and put him in a Sit and Wait position until the person has passed safely by without muddy paw marks round his ankles.

Your first few walks with puppy should be short and, above all, interesting. It should certainly not be one long nag from you for puppy to stop pulling or diving about or barking. You must gain your puppy's interest by sharing and taking part in this new found world. Katy, my young Labrador puppy, was quite worried about her first walk, but then she's a very sensitive dog and needed much encouragement along the pavements. Luckily, it was autumn and leaves were blowing across her paws. Her fear of the unknown was suddenly forgotten as she chased the leaves along the pavement. I encouraged this by picking up leaves and throwing them in front of her. She was so engrossed in her leaf-chasing, that large lorries and buses passing by were not even given a second glance.

Duration and frequency of your puppy's exercise

A young puppy is far better exercised frequently. A few minutes two or three times a day is far better than an hour occasionally. It will break him in gradually to the new rules and regulations of walking along the pavements and will not tire his brain or his body. It is impossible to advise you how long and how often you should be exercising your dog, for every breed and every dog within that breed varies. But most puppies will get ample exercise in your own garden if you take the time to play with them. The same rules apply to free-running your puppy. Little and often should be your rule.

CHAPTER 7

FREE RUNS

The biggest problem most dog owners have is getting their dogs to return to them on command once the dog is off the lead. But so many owners cause their own problems on this exercise, I'm not surprised their dogs don't wish to return to them. Let us first view the faults, in the hope of preventing you from making the same mistakes.

Why your dog won't come back to you

The first and simplest reason your dog will not return to you on command is that you haven't trained him thoroughly in the garden. If he won't come when called in the confined space of his own home, he certainly won't in the freedom of the fields. In the main, owners with untrained dogs are full of excuses. Week after week, owners come to me saying that the methods don't work and the dog will not do such-and-such an exercise. What they really mean is that they are unable to train their dog. Far too many people walk about like dead lettuce leaves, talking to their dogs in uninterested undertones. It's a wonder half the dog population don't shoot themselves with sheer boredom! The first law in dog training is to get your dog interested in you and to sound enthusiastic enough for your dog to leave his exciting smells and return to you immediately. I think nothing of leaping up and down in the park, clapping my hands in the air, shouting, rolling on the grass and pretending to have the most marvellous game. That never fails to get my dogs racing back to me.

The second most common fault is that at some time the owner has made it unpleasant when the dog has returned, either by nagging at him to sit, or telling him off because when he returned he jumped all over them. If you must adorn yourself in finery and best clothes before exercising your dog, you deserve muddy paw marks all over you. The best way to deter your puppy from returning to you is to nag at him for jumping up, or even being violent with a young puppy and hitting him on return because he didn't come back at the first call. Dogs have very long memories and once you've hit a dog for returning to you, he will never forget it.

From my five dogs, I can tell you of various reasons for a dog not returning to his owner. Katy, as a young puppy on her first few walks in the park was fascinated by strangers and would often follow them, regardless of my calls. I admit to being quite annoyed about this and my first instinct was to run after her and lecture her in no uncertain terms about the penalties for disobedience. Luckily, I thought carefully first. Katy was a very sensitive puppy. If I were to use harsh words while she was with a stranger, would she think strangers were something to be afraid of? Remembering that young puppies can't concentrate for long and have only room in their little minds for one thing—and that once it's off their owner it has to be gained by physical contact—I approached her quietly and carefully and stroked her, spoke her name a few times and then backed off, calling her and offering a titbit. She immediately forgot the stranger and ran back with me to the other dogs. This happened two or three times and each time I repeated my tactic. Within a week or two, Katy would return to me immediately. Her name called in an enthusiastic manner meant I had a titbit in my hand for her and, as far as Labradors are concerned, food overrides everything.

Food is certainly Buttons' main interest in life. She came to us at a year old, more or less untrained. She is the total opposite to Katy, completely dominant. In fact, Buttons is the nearest thing I've ever met to a chauvinist dog. Given the opportunity, she would drag on the lead, bark and growl at passing dogs and run off in the fields. Needless to say, she is never given the opportunity to misbehave. With Buttons, I constantly think ahead to be sure of being one step in front of her. Many dogs like Buttons have what I call an obedience barrier. Within so many yards of their owners these dogs will always obey, but beyond a certain point they are completely deaf to any commands. If you are the owner of one of these dogs, you must assess the distance of your obedience barrier and constantly keep your dog within those bounds. Buttons will always return if she's within her barrier. Once over the line she is gone, off in search of food. Despite the fact that Buttons is always vying with me for leadership and, given the opportunity, will be disobedient, she is extremely intelligent and watches me constantly while on our walks through the park and the woods. She looks for a lapse of concentration on my part and then she instantly makes for the nearest rubbish tip hidden away in the woods, where she will forage for what she thinks of as tasty morsels. No amount of chastising or threatening works. The only thing to do, instantly and always, is the offer of food. I constantly carry a pocket of titbits and keep Buttons within range.

Dogs like Buttons are much harder to control than those like Teak, our German shorthaired pointer, who will wander completely out of sight but have no obedience barrier and will return instantly on a call or a whistle. A 'Good girl' of praise is quite enough for her. All my dogs, except Buttons, came to us as puppies and were never allowed to be disobedient and were trained correctly from an early age, so problems like the ones I have with

Buttons never developed. Every dog is trainable but it is far easier to start from puppyhood.

The third reason your dog will not return to you is that he is far more interested in playing with other dogs. In the case of a male, he will probably spend much of his life, if left entire, in search of a female companion. You could never break an entire dog of wanting to seek a bitch and, therefore, it is far easier for you, and kinder for your male dog, if you have him castrated. I do not make the sweeping statement that all male dogs will constantly run after bitches, not at all. It depends entirely on their temperament and your ability as a dog trainer, but I am trying to point out to you the easiest and best methods of having a well-behaved dog.

Now I have informed you of all the faults and problems that you could have, let us begin correctly so that none of these faults occur.

Where and when to exercise your dog

Try to choose a secluded, grassy area for your first lesson with your puppy. Do not train in children's play areas or let your dog run there. My own local council have provided exercising areas for dogs, plus toilet facilities. This is marvellous and I wish every other council were as considerate. It would prevent fouling of play-areas and pavements and would, I am sure, lead to more conscientious dog-ownership. Choose a time when your puppy will not be distracted by lots of people or strange dogs. Take pockets full of titbits and your puppy's favourite toy, and add to this a long lead. An old washing line will do, or a special long lead you can acquire from your pet shop for the very purpose of training your puppy to return on command. Give puppy his signal which means he is released. I use the words Off you go, and give him a few yards of lead. As he reaches the end of this lead, give him a friendly little tug and your command, Come. If he returns to you immediately, be liberal with your titbits and have a game with him. If, on the other hand, he's far too engrossed in wonderful smells arising from the grass, make your tug stronger and be firm with your Come command. Make your puppy come to you. However he reacts, even if he has no desire to come back to you, do make a fuss of him once he's in your reach. Give him the titbits and have a game. A small puppy, or even an adult dog, will respond far better to the recalls if you get down to his level. Often the small and more sensitive kind of dog will be afraid to come back to you as you tower above him, as he feels this could be a threat. Be careful with your arms and hands when encouraging your puppy to come to you. Don't flail them about in the air trying to grab at him. Keep them still as you offer out the titbit. As puppy comes closer, gently stroke him, and if you wish to put him back on his lead take hold of his collar quietly.

I must remind you here that every dog is different, depending on his

The Recall on a long lead
TOP Teaching the Recall in a park
BOTTOM LEFT Bring the dog to you with plenty of encouragement
BOTTOM RIGHT Do not shout at your dog for jumping up on Recall.
He will think you are annoyed that he has come to you

breed, temperament and overriding instincts. Therefore, you must use your own common sense of how best to deal with an unresponsive puppy. If puppy constantly ignores the Come command and the tug at his lead, you must be more forceful. Make the command firmer and the tug stronger, until the puppy has no option but to return to you immediately. You must never revert to screams and yells or threats of violence. You are in full control of the situation as puppy is on a long lead. Firmness in the voice should be used on your initial command but, as puppy comes towards you, your voice should be light and enthusiastic. As your puppy responds to your commands, the lead should be made longer and longer until puppy feels he's completely free. But do remember that your puppy is bound to be engrossed in new and interesting smells and if he sees another dog, his instinct to go and play will be overwhelming and, as in the street, I advise that you let him play with other dogs and call him in frequently to give him a titbit. If, every time your puppy comes back to you, you put him on a lead and take him home, this will give him the impression that he's not allowed to run about and enjoy himself and will be very reluctant to return to you, knowing it means the end of his free run. Call him in frequently while he's having a good time with other dogs. Make it plain that you're delighted to see him, giving him a titbit and a fuss and let him go again. Only when you are totally confident that your puppy will return to you under different circumstances .should you let him off his long line completely. Depending on your puppy, you may have to use this long line once or twice a week to give him a reminder that he must come immediately when called. But if this behaviour pattern is instilled into a young dog, and every time he returns to you it is pleasant to be with you, you should have no problems in the future. If you have tried to rush the exercise by letting your puppy off too soon or by getting annoyed with him when he doesn't return, then you are making your dog untrustworthy. The only time I ever tell a dog off for not returning to me is when I can go up to the dog without him seeing me. Sometimes, my Labrador, Buttons, is engrossed in some tasty morsel. I then creep up behind her, take hold of the scruff of her neck and really give her a good lecture about listening to me and not foraging for food. I then insist that she walks with me for a while, close at heel, letting her out a little further and a little further as the minutes go by, but frequently calling her in to give her titbits.

Your visits to the park or fields should be frequent for short runs and the more you can play and talk to your puppy while he's off the lead and running free, the more he'll want to be with you. I make my visits to the park as enjoyable for the dogs as possible, always taking a rubber ring or ball that they can play retrieve games with. This way, they always return to me, for I'm the one who instigates the games and puts the fun into everything they do. If you're having no joy with your puppy, if he's not interested in returning to you or playing games with you, look to yourself. Think for a moment about your friends and who you like to be with. I prefer to be with someone who's lighthearted and always making jokes and laughing. Those people who constantly moan and nag about aches and pains or bills they've received recently are avoided by me. Your puppy must feel exactly the same about personalities, so I'm afraid that if you are a moaner and a nagger, you will have to try hard to change your temperament, or not have a dog in the first place.

CHAPTER 8

STAYS

A good reason for teaching Stay

I am sure that you will find all the exercises extremely useful if only to teach your dog discipline and self-control, but there are other practical reasons for teaching them. I remember once when my daughter Kerensa was a toddler and I was taking Bracken, Mocha and Buttons out for a walk. Unbeknown to me Kerensa had pocketed a tennis ball on the way out and before I realised what was happening she was bouncing the tennis ball on the pavement, and it rolled away into the road. Kerensa ran after it. Instinctively I dropped the dog leads, told them to Sit and Stay and rushed after Kerensa. Needless to say, all was well. I was able to retrieve her without a scratch, secure in the knowledge that the three dogs were still sitting and staying on the pavement.

Since that time I have practised my Sit-Stays while I run after Kerensa, as dogs will often think this is a game and immediately run after their owner.

Sit-Stay

The Stay command is taught in the same manner as Wait. But Stay should mean to your puppy that he must not move off the spot until you return to him and give a release command. Do not teach Stays and Waits together. I prefer to do small exercises all through the day, never linking up two different things at the same time. I may teach a Wait and have a game with my puppy and a little later on in the day I will teach collar-and-lead work, and so on. In this way, your puppy will not be confused and he will enjoy his training. Remember, every new command you're teaching puppy is a foreign word. You must give him time to understand. Only while puppy is interested in your training lessons will he learn. It is pointless to spend half an hour teaching him Stays. He will be bored and uninterested. A few minutes here and there is far better.

With puppy sitting on your left-hand side, give him a firm but quiet Stay command. Do not use his name. Remember his name is an indication for him to come to you and we don't want that. Take a small pace to your right and then immediately return to your puppy, kneel down and praise

The Sit-Stay
TOP LEFT Give a calm quiet Stay command
TOP RIGHT Take one pace to the side
RIGHT Return almost immediately

him. Do not make the mistake of stretching your hand back as you return to puppy to give him praise. You will only be teaching him to be unsteady and to jump towards you as you return. Puppy must be taught from the very beginning that he must stay in the position you have left him until you return and physically stroke him and give him the release command. If your puppy moves, even if it only be a front paw in your direction, quietly put him back exactly where you left him and repeat your Stay command.

As with every other exercise I have explained, you must take into account your puppy's temperament. A sensitive puppy will worry that you are going to leave him and, naturally, want to follow you. You must not be harsh with him, but calm. Stroke him when you're giving him the command of Stay, to reassure him. After all, you are only taking one pace to the right and then returning to him immediately. This will give him confidence. The more dominant puppy will want to be off and do his own thing and should be treated accordingly. The dominant puppy will not require stroking when giving the command and if he attempts to move away from you, be very firm when putting him back into the Sit-Stay position.

Stays must be done on the spot with you only one step away. It is pointless to make a lot of distance between you and puppy. Once you are out of arms reach, you have no control over him. If you rush to the other end of the room, shouting at your puppy to stay and he gets up, you cannot correct him. This will give puppy the idea that he can be disobedient once you are but a few paces away and you will upset a more sensitive puppy by constantly shouting at him to stay. So don't be tempted to rush this exercise.

If puppy lies down when you've left him in a Sit-Stay, don't be tempted to leave him. You have given a command of Sit, so you must ensure it is carried out. Put him back into the Sit, gently. If he rolls and wants to play, just walk round him for a moment before putting him back into the Sit. Only when you know puppy has a grasp of this new command can you begin to extend your distance and time. When you can take two paces away at the side of your puppy and count five seconds, you will know he is beginning to grasp the meaning of this new word. Then you can extend this to three or four paces to the side and ten seconds. You should begin to walk slowly around your puppy in the Sit-Stay. It is quite acceptable to repeat the word Stay, but do not use your dog's name. This will be an indication for him to get up and come to you.

Once your circling has been achieved in the house, you can do your Stays in the garden, and next into the park where there'll be the distraction of other people and dogs. Always keep your puppy on a lead so that you have full control and he cannot be disobedient. Only when your puppy is absolutely steady in the Sit-Stay in the park can you begin to extend your distance. But if you think that puppy will move, keep him on a lead so that you have full control. The worst possible thing you can do in this exercise is to scream and shout at your dog to stay or sit when he moves and you're not in a position to correct him. This will only put him off doing this exercise and confuse him and you will then need to go back to the very beginning and start all over again.

The golden rule of training is never to let puppy make mistakes. My own Labradors love doing Stays, probably because, as a breed, they are basically idle, but I did come across one or two problems with Katy. While I was in full control of the situation teaching her Stays at home or in the park, everything went well and Katy had every confidence in this new command. But once she was old enough to be entered in Obedience shows, her Stays became a misery to her and, for a while, I couldn't understand where I had made my mistakes. Each time I took her into the Stay ring, her ears went back and her body went stiff and I could tell from the expression on her face that she was extremely worried about the exercise and, although she never actually broke the Stay command at a show, she was never relaxed or happy once put into a Sit or Down-Stay.

After one or two shows, I realised why Katy was afraid. Although I gave a quiet and gentle Stay command, many of the other competitors close to me were shouting at their dogs. Naturally, Katy felt that they were all shouting at her. I fervently believe that if you need to scream and yell commands at your dog, you have not trained him correctly. Dogs have very sensitive hearing and tend to shut themselves off to loud noises. The yell and scream owners are achieving nothing except a disobedient dog. As I had no control or power to stop these owners shouting, I had to be more gentle and reassuring with Katy and I now tend to pick my place in the Stay ring very carefully, next to people who won't yell at their dogs.

Down-Stay

Once you have achieved the Sit-Stay, the Down-Stay will be very simple. Your dog now understands this new command. Put him in the Down and give him the Stay. He should not attempt to move if your Sit-Stay has been trained thoroughly.

Stand-Stay

You may wish to teach your dog to stay in a Stand position, for grooming purposes, or if you intend to show him in the future. This exercise should be approached with more care, as most dogs left in a Stand-Stay will worry and often go into a Sit or a Down position. You must not attempt to leave your dog's side for the first few lessons of Stand. Give him this new word Stand and stroke him gently under the tummy, so that holding this

The Stand-Stay
Reassure your dog by stroking him during this exercise

position is a pleasure. Give him the Stay command and walk slowly round him, stroking him all the time on his head, his chest, his back and underneath the tummy. You are boosting his confidence and making the Stand a pleasure. If he moves a paw or tries to turn with you, place him gently back and stroke his tummy, repeating the word Stand and immediately you walk round him, repeat the word Stay. When your puppy is quite happy with this new position, you can then begin to leave him a pace or two, but always stay close at hand so that if you can see your puppy moving, you can immediately put your hand underneath him and reassure, and repeat your Stand-Stay command. I can see no reason for achieving a distance in a Stand-Stay unless you wish to do competition obedience.

Stop there

Because of the many years I worked and relied on Emma, I would feel quite naked if I had to walk down the road dogless. So my whole way of life is centred around the dogs. Shopping, for instance, is only another excuse for a dog walk, but in recent years, shopping with a dog has become more and more difficult because of the ever-increasing 'No Dogs' signs. I realised that if I wanted to take the dogs shopping with me, I had to find and teach a new command. I felt it would be cruel to leave my dog in a Sit-Stay when entering a shop. I may be as long as twenty minutes to half an hour and it would be unkind to leave a dog for that length of time in a Stay position, so I added the command Stop there to my dogs' knowledge of the English language. Stop there means that they must stay on the spot I've left them but they can sit or stand or move around. I would always advise you to secure your dog to a nearby post or hook provided by the shop. However reliable you feel your dog to be, something could happen. He could be attacked by another dog, jumped on by a strange cat, lured away by a toddler with an ice-cream or frightened by the back-firing of a car.

Your first training lesson should take place in the actual spot you need to visit most frequently, i.e. the local shop. Ensure that your dog has plenty of room to move about and that he will not choke himself because you have tied him up on too short a lead. Tell him to Stop there, that you are going into the shop and you won't be long. Move out of sight of your puppy just for a moment. If all goes well, return and praise. If puppy begins to howl and bark and drag at his collar, rush back to him and tell him to Stop there and that you will not accept that type of behaviour, and try again. Whatever you are teaching your dog, force must be met with force. If puppy constantly yaps and barks and misbehaves, then you must dash back to him and firmly tell him to Stop there, using, if necessary, a physical reprimand by taking hold of the scruff of his neck and firmly repeating your command. If you give in now, you will have a problem dog that you cannot take shopping with you and he will suffer being left at home because you have not had the patience to train him correctly in the first place.

Warning

Never tie your dog up on a check-chain collar. This can be very dangerous. The more the dog pulls, the more the collar tightens and if by any chance he gets his legs entangled in the lead he could literally choke himself to death.

CHAPTER 9

THE SIX-MONTH SUMMARY

At this stage in your puppy's training he should be around the age of five to six months. Remember, the more you can teach him before he reaches the age of six months, the easier and pleasanter your life will be together. You should still be taking puppy out on a soft leather collar and I advise for your comfort, a long, soft leather lead. A chain lead will cut into your hands. Rope and nylon tend to burn. I see so many owners of young puppies with chain leads because their puppy has chewed the soft leather ones. Puppies usually turn to chew their leather lead for two reasons: either they are bored, or they wish to distract their owner. It is a very simple habit to stop. With a gentle tug, bring the lead downwards through your puppy's mouth and give him the command to Leave. Most owners with chain leads just have not had the patience to repeat this exercise over and over again. Their usual excuse is, 'Oh, I tried that, and it didn't work.' Most people believe that telling or showing a puppy once will train it for life. If I am given a new machine, whether it be a tape recorder, a typewriter or a computer, it will take me some time to understand the workings completely. How can we be naïve enough to believe that our puppies are far more intelligent than us and will pick something up in one lesson?

The bone test

Now is the time to discover who is Boss. Your puppy will benefit from having a raw marrow bone and you will learn a lot. Never give puppy cooked or chop bones or poultry bones—only the raw marrow or knuckle bone. He will keep himself amused for hours and if he is still teething, it will help him discard any loose teeth. Once your puppy is engrossed in his bone, does he growl at your approach? The well-trained, well-matched puppy should be quite happy to relinquish his bone to you. Any sign of aggression should be stopped instantly. If you fail to act now, you will have serious problems in the future. A dog who is aggressive over his bone is dominant and firmly believes that he is Boss. I actually know owners who are afraid of their dogs and dare not approach them when they have a bone or a toy, for fear of being bitten. This is an appalling situation and should never arise.

Lead Chewing
TOP Step to the side
BOTTOM Then take the lead
downwards to stop puppy
biting his lead

Act quickly

What do you do if your dog does growl while eating his bone? Act immediately and with great determination. Seize your dog by the scruff of his neck and take the bone from him, telling him that you will not stand for this disgusting behaviour. Still keeping a firm grip on your puppy, place the bone on the floor and give him the command to Leave. If puppy obeys your command, pick the bone up and give it him, stroking him all the time. Repeat these actions frequently while your dog is chewing the bone until there is no sign of aggression whatsoever on your approach.

If your puppy is dominant and continues to try to snatch his bone off the floor and growl, be more dominant with him. Insist that he sits and leaves his bone until you return it to him. You must not resort to physical violence, kicking out or hitting your puppy. If he does have the slightest tendency towards aggression, he will bite in self-defence and you can hardly blame him for that. You must take physical action by the scruff of the neck only. This never hurts a dog, just his pride, and asserts the fact that you are Boss.

Understanding your puppy's temperament

I have never known a puppy yet who will not try to get his own way. Even the most submissive puppy will try it on and the technique you should use depends on the temperament of your puppy. It varies from outward aggression to plain stupidity, where the puppy sits and pretends he does not understand what you want, to the very submissive puppy showing fear when asked to do something he is set against. I admit, it is often very difficult to read the signs and you need to have a full understanding of your puppy to know what action to take. Katy is a very submissive puppy and would no more think of growling at me than fly. Nevertheless, at the age of nine months she began to feel the need to assert her authority and get her own way. She would often cringe and lower her body to the ground when asked to do something quite mundane. At first, I misread these signs and always reassured her, thinking that something I hadn't seen or heard had worried her.

The cringing became more frequent and I was beginning to think I had a nervous dog on my hands and yet, as a puppy, she'd been bold and friendly and game for anything. I gave this action very careful thought and realised that the more I sympathised with her and encouraged her not to be afraid, the more she cringed. Inside, she was probably laughing her paws off. She'd got me just where she wanted. A cringe brought caresses and sympathy and lots of attention, so she did it all the more. Once I realised what was happening, the next cringe was met very sternly on my part with, 'Katy, I will not stand for that. There is nothing to be afraid of, now don't be silly!' Within a split second she had changed to the friendly, bold, bouncing dog she'd always been. She knew I'd found her out and she never did it again.

Mocha, on the other hand, feigns stupidity, which is not very difficult for her. She's the nearest thing I've ever met to a backward Labrador. She has the sweetest disposition and a tail that never stops wagging. But there was a time in her training when I began to believe she was deaf. No matter how I encouraged or commanded, she would sit totally ignoring me, and yet the slightest sound of a food bowl being placed on the floor would bring her at top speed. I simply proved to Mocha that whatever I told her to do she must and no amount of feigning stupidity would get her out of it.

Teak, our German shorthaired pointer, is the type of dog who feels she can get away with blue murder. Having just stolen an apple pie from the kitchen and eaten the lot in one gobble, she will come to me, her stumpy tail wagging and her body circling, denying all knowledge that there was an apple pie and, even if there was, she would never have eaten it. How could I believe such a terrible thing of her? It must be one of the other dogs.

I can show you dozens of dogs who lead their owners a dance by putting on various emotions to achieve supremacy. Bracken will put on what I call his 'rose petal expression' when he thinks I am going to tell him off for some misdemeanour. His ears turn back and round and remind me of the shape of rose petals. He has an extremely worried expression on his face and always walks quietly up to me and pushes his nose under my arm, as if asking forgiveness. He feels, if he shows submission and sorrow for what he's done, I wouldn't dream of telling him off. To be perfectly honest with you, it usually works. Well, I'm only human!

Buttons is the most dominant dog I've owned and probably, with a less experienced handler, she could have been quite a problem. She came to us at a year old and within a few days tried to assert her authority. One evening, when it was 'everybody out' time—my dogs understand that phrase, it means the last trot round the garden before bedtime—Buttons was snoozing in her bed. I called the command again. She took no notice. Giving her the benefit of the doubt, I approached and stroked her, repeating the command. She growled. If I'd have made the mistake of backing off and being afraid, I would have been under Buttons' paw for the rest of my life. But I didn't. I acted with speed and alacrity, taking hold of the scruff of her neck. 'You horrible dog,' I told her, in the nearest tone to a growling voice I could achieve. I showed her to the back door and said firmly, 'Everybody out includes Buttons!' When I opened the back door a moment or two later to let the dogs back in, Buttons came with tail wagging and immediately rolled on the floor in a submissive position. From that day forth, it was acknowledged that I was Boss.

I can show you quite a few dogs who put on a limp when their owner

is taking them somewhere they don't like. In my opinion, dogs are far more intelligent than most people would like to admit. I haven't met one yet who doesn't have a conscience or can't work out how to get his own way. I have heard many experienced dog handlers state categorically that dogs have no reasoning power. I feel very fortunate to have worked with a guide-dog like Emma for so many years, for I can state just as categorically that they do.

Bracken has a vast amount of reasoning power and will sit carefully working a scheme out before he takes action. One evening, Mocha and Teak were playing with a squeaky toy that Bracken desperately wanted for his own. He tried the usual acts, grabbing the toy off them or jumping on them and growling but nothing worked. Mocha and Teak managed to keep it in their possession. So, Bracken sat back with a look of deep thought in his eyes, then he suddenly took action. He ran from the lounge, down the hall to the front door and began barking furiously. Mocha and Teak dropped the squeaky toy and followed suit. There was, of course, no one there, but before Teak and Mocha had worked this out, Bracken had doubled back into the lounge and taken possession of the squeaky toy.

Bracken pretending there is someone at the door

CHAPTER 10

FAST DOWNS AND SEND-AWAYS

The Down position is the one exercise most dogs hate doing. In the wild, a canine lying down denotes submission and this instinct is still very strong in our pet dogs. The exception to this rule is the working collie, who will drop at a whistle when herding sheep. But if you watch the collie at work very carefully, you will realise that his hunting instinct is to the fore, and down he may be but every muscle in his body is alert, ready for the spring. When using and training working dogs, we are only channelling their basic instinct. The guide-dog is a good example of this, for all a guide-dog is learning is self-preservation, but he is extending his own body range, taller and wider, to encompass his human being. Of course, the training of guide-dogs is far more detailed and complicated. That is a simple explanation of how man can train dog to work for him. Whatever we're training our dogs to do, we must think of their basic instinct and work round it. Often, no amount of force and commanding will encourage a dog to go into the Down position, especially at a distance from his owner. The most effective way to teach your puppy Fast Downs is to make it a game.

Fast Downs with fun

The one thing you should keep in mind is your puppy's comfort, and encouraging him to do Fast Downs will be far easier on a soft surface, a carpet or the lawn. Before I train my puppies to do anything, I try to put myself in their place and think how they feel and I know I would hate lying down on concrete. You will need your puppy on a lead to begin your Fast Down training. A toy or a favourite titbit should be offered as a reward. With puppy on your left, hold the lead in your right hand down at puppy's height, just a few inches in front of his nose, with your titbit or his toy clasped in your right hand. Then, you must run as fast as you can, ensuring that puppy wants to get his toy or titbit from your right hand. The speed is essential, for all you will need to do then is catch puppy off-balance to put him in the Down position. This is very simple when he is trotting or running. This method is virtually impossible from the Stand position.

84

Fast Downs
TOP LEFT Run with puppy
TOP RIGHT Hand on his shoulders
and lead down
LEFT Play with puppy when he
is in the down position

Give a firm Down command, bringing your right hand, with lead and titbit, to the ground. It is very difficult to do this if you are still upright. You will find it smoother and simpler to go down on one knee and as you are going down, place your left hand on puppy's shoulder, give a gentle push away from you and down. As soon as puppy is in the Down position, release the titbit or toy from your hand and have a game with him. If you need to force your puppy into the Down position, you are doing it wrong. You have probably stopped before putting puppy into the Down. It must be a smooth and speedy movement and this exercise cannot be carried out correctly if you walk. You must trot or, preferably, run.

I am sure that if you were not fit when you began to train your puppy, you are either fighting fit now or a complete wreck of a human being. I don't feel I've achieved anything after a training lesson unless I'm totally exhausted and have run and jumped about with my dog. I have many dog owners who only come to my training classes once because they are not prepared to put any effort or enthusiasm into their puppy's training. I feel so sorry for these dogs, who retreat from my class, tail between their legs, thoroughly miserable, dragged along by just as miserable-looking owners who feel their dogs should be obedient without any application on their part. Teaching Fast Downs is a sure way of shaking you out of your reverie and, unless you put the magic ingredients into this exercise—speed, encouragement and enthusiasm—you will get nowhere at all.

Once your puppy has an understanding of this new exercise and begins to go into the Down position as soon as your right hand lowers to the ground, you can extend your distance with this Fast Down. After a week or two, you should be able to do this exercise without puppy's lead or your hand touching him and just holding your hand in front of him, offering a toy or titbit and giving the Down command. You can then extend this to throwing the toy or titbit once puppy has gone down. This will keep him alert and watchful and speedy in obeying your Down. Now you and puppy are ready to extend this exercise into a Send-Away. You may think sending your dog away from you is a little pointless. Not at all. You are teaching puppy that, even when he's running from you, he must be alert to your commands.

Some good reasons for teaching the Send-Away

A dog who is taught the Send-Away exercise correctly will drop into a Down position when he's running away from his owner. You may find yourself in a situation where you need to be in total control of your dog once he's off the lead and a recall would be dangerous. For example, you are in a field in the country, your dog is running free and out of nowhere appears a flock of sheep. A farmer has the right to shoot any dog he sees running near his livestock. The farmer may not have seen you, or know that your dog is under control. A recall, in this situation, could give him the impression that the dog is running after livestock and not back to his owner. The fastest and safest way to protect your dog's life is to drop him on the spot into a Down position. You can then walk up to him and put him on the lead.

Another, more common, occurrence is around your own home. However careful you are, there is a chance that puppy may escape from his own garden. Someone may have left the gate open or your puppy could find his way out through a gap in the fence. What would you do if you saw him on the opposite side of the main road? A recall would be dangerous in this situation. He could be killed crossing back to you. He may even endanger human life. If your dog will obey the distance Down command, he will drop and wait for you to reach him. Many dogs who have an obedience barrier and will not return to a recall when running away from their owners will, instinctively, drop on command if the Send-Away has been taught thoroughly and correctly.

Teaching the Send-Away

As with all training exercise, the beginning of the Send-Away can be taught in your own back garden. Choose a spot in your garden to mark where you wish puppy to run away to and go down. This can be the line-post, the shed, the corner of the hedge, or by just marking out an area with plant pots in a square that you wish your puppy to run to. Start a few yards away from your chosen spot with puppy sitting on your left. Then, with much enthusiasm and excitement, tell him he's going to do Send-Aways. Run with him up the garden to the spot, telling him the command all the way, 'Away . . . away.' As soon as you reach the spot, put puppy into the Down position. Make a lot of fuss and have a game with him before you repeat this exercise. You will need to do this exercise and run with your dog quite a number of times before he gets the idea. You will know when he understands the words, for he will race you up the garden to his spot and, as soon as he reaches it, give him the Down command. When all is going well, you can extend your distance further and further back from his elected spot. In the park, you can use your coat, or bag, as a Send-Away mark for your dog to run to and, as your puppy has more confidence in this new exercise, you can extend the distance.

You may find, after a time, puppy will not go down on command, in which case you must revert to running to the spot with him and physically putting him into the Down position. If he is not interested in running away from you then you have not made the game interesting enough and must go back to running all the way with him, giving your Away command with

The Send-Away
TOP Encourage the dog to run
CENTRE . . . past the markers
BOTTOM Put him into a Down
and reward him with his toy

excitement and enthusiasm, not forgetting your reward of fuss and a game once he has reached his spot and gone into the Down.

I find, with all training exercises, that my dogs need refresher courses and as soon as I can see they lack enthusiasm, or the will to please on any exercise, I go back to the very beginning and re-train them. You must never feel despondent when you find that puppy will not obey a command that he has been well taught. Even the Supreme Obedience Champions of Crufts need constant reminders and encouragement to be obedient. Don't be afraid to re-train an exercise completely and always be ready to give your puppy constant reminders by physically showing him what you require.

After that exhausting chapter, I think you are entitled to put your feet up for half an hour or so while you read through the next chapter.

CHAPTER 11

TEACHING SOMETHING DIFFERENT

Assuming that you have had great success in the training of your puppy, it would be a shame to stop now. You have obviously built up a good relationship with him and, once this is gained between dog and human being, there are no limits to how much you can train him. I believe the more you teach your dog the more intelligent he will become. Teaching a dog tricks is often frowned upon by the more serious dog trainers. I think they hold a picture in their minds of the old circus dog with a frill round his neck, dancing on his hind legs. My interpretation of teaching a dog tricks is a little different from that and I can assure you, from my own past experience, that a dog loves doing new and more interesting things. Take into account the type of dog you have. With my own dogs, for instance, it is Bracken who loves to learn and he gets so excited when he knows it's trick-teaching time. He rushes around to grab cushions off the settee or towels off the kitchen rail to bring me as an offering in exchange for a trick lesson.

Start with a full understanding of your dog's characteristics. For example, Bracken would hate learning to jump. Yet Teak would jump fences all day long just for the sheer joy of it. So, it is up to you to find your dog's natural attributes and work on them. Before I began training Bracken his tricks, I thought carefully of what he would like to do. He's a very vocal dog. He loves fetching and carrying. But, basically, he's idle.

Barking on command

Teaching your dog to speak on command can be very useful. Many people have told me that their dogs will not bark when someone knocks at the door and, as dogs must be considered one of the biggest deterrents to burglars, a dog that doesn't bark can be a bit of a disappointment. Although I must admit to you that I spent two years trying to teach Emma to bark, without success. I tried everything, but nothing on earth would induce her to say a word and she was over four years old when she emitted her first bark at a knock on the door. From that first bark, she became the perfect house-dog, knowing when to bark and when to stop.

But how do you teach your dog to bark on command? You must be observant and find out what makes your puppy bark. If it's someone at the door, fine, your training will be very easy. He may bark with excitement when you're playing with him. He could bark for food. Most dogs will bark for something. Find out what it is and use it. Each time he barks give him a command. I use the word Speak. Praise the dog immediately and offer a titbit. How fast your dog learns this new command all depends on you. If you can be there each time he barks, to praise, give the command and a titbit, he will learn all the quicker. As you will have gathered from this description of training your dog to speak, you cannot force your dog to learn tricks—it happens from natural situations. Once he understands what the command Speak means, you can then control it to how many times he barks and when to stop. A dog that starts barking and will not stop can easily be controlled by giving another command. I use Be quiet. Give this command and offer a titbit and praise, or play with your dog with his favourite toy. He will then begin to associate the words Be quiet with something pleasant and be only too keen to comply. So, training your dog to speak on command will also solve your problem if you have a noisy dog. It is pointless to shout and reprimand a dog for barking. He doesn't understand what he's doing wrong. So actually teaching him the word to bark and teaching him the command to be quiet will clarify this situation to him.

Teaching your dog to retrieve

Teaching the retrieve to a dog who isn't retrieve-minded can be a long and painful process; painful for the owner, I might add, not for the dog. So I advise you that, unless your dog is a natural retriever or you specifically want him to fetch things for you, forget this exercise and find something else your dog's good at. Remember, all these extra things you are teaching your pet should be pleasurable both to you and him and if you find that your dog isn't enjoying the exercises, forget it. If you've played with your dog from being a young puppy then the chances are that he will retrieve. Throw him an old sock or a pair of knotted tights and give him a command to fetch. He will no doubt race off and pick up the article and then run about with it, with no intention of bringing it back to you. Now is the time to find out if your training has really worked. Does he respond to the command Come? If he returns to you with the article still in his mouth, you are half-way there. Take hold of the article and ask your dog to Give. If he hangs on for grim death, you must exchange his precious toy for something else; a titbit or another toy that he can play with. Once your dog has it in his mind that bringing something to you brings rewards, your retrieve training will be simple. The dog who rushes off and has no intention of sharing his prize with you should be re-taught the Come command. Often, this type of dog will respond to the recall but will drop the article, in which case run back and pick it up yourself, throw it in the air a few times until he takes hold of it again, then immediately swop it for a titbit. For the dog who shows no inclination whatsoever to run after a toy then forget it and train him something different.

Of course, any dog can be taught anything with time and patience and the right technique but I don't wish this book to be a bore. I want you and your dog to enjoy everything, so I would much rather you find things you can do together, without a lot of effort on your part and with a lot of enjoyment on your dog's part. But, for those of you who have a natural retrieving dog, you can have enormous fun by not only teaching him the simple retrieve but also by teaching scent discrimination. Nearly all these exercises can be taught in the comfort of your own lounge while you're watching television. All you need to do is hide one of your articles, a glove or a sock, for example. (Do make sure the sock has been washed or it won't only be the dog that's doing scent discrimination!) Hide your article behind a chair or under a table. Give your dog your hand to smell and the word Scent. You must then show him how the game is played by rushing about, using the word Scent frequently and looking round, pretending that you have forgotten where your article is. If your dog spies it before you and takes hold of it, show enormous excitement and ask him to bring it to you. Don't forget to swop it for a titbit or his toy. If you find it first, show the puppy the article, repeating the command Scent and encourage him to pick it up and bring it to you.

All the dogs that I have taught this game to are so keen to play that they come and nudge and then dash about. This can be then extended into the garden or the park and fields. You can casually drop your glove while you're walking along. A few paces later, give your dog the command Scent and run back with him showing enthusiasm until he spots the glove and brings it back to you. This is an extremely useful exercise, as I have often dropped a glove or even house keys and I've been able to send my dog in search of them. As one of dogs' greatest attributes must be their sense of smell, it is a shame not to use it and show them what fun it can be.

Jumping

If you own the energetic type of dog, he will no doubt love to race and jump and a dog that is full of beans and wants to be on the go all day long can often be satisfied by five or ten minutes' jumping in his own garden. But, as with all things you are training your dog, you should show him how to do it. Whatever you do, don't put a six-foot jump up in the garden and try and clear it yourself, unless, that is, you're an Olympic hurdler. To begin with, use a very small jump which can be simply made. I usually put the handle of a yard brush across two buckets, giving me about eighteen inches in height. With your dog on a loose lead, run at the jump with him, showing great enthusiasm. Be ready to let the lead go if your dog pulls back or refuses to go over the jump. You may have misjudged him—he could be just like my Bracken and have no intention of exerting his surplus energy, in which case you will have to teach him to play 'dead dog'. But if your dog comes with you over the jump and shows he's enjoying it, continue. Give him a command. I use the word Over. If he revels in this type of exercise, you will only need to show him once or twice. You can then let him off the lead, give him the command Over and off he'll go. You can then move the height of your jumps very slowly upwards. Never ask him to jump more than three feet and if your dog ever shows caution or worry at the sight of a jump, forget it.

There is now much more interest shown throughout the country in the agility side of dog training and it can be enormous fun for both dog and handler. If your dog loves jumping and you enjoy training him, find a local dog training club that has an agility course. I can guarantee you and the dog will have enormous pleasure in this pursuit.

Just for the fun of it

I have taught Bracken to do lots of little tricks, just for the fun of it. For instance, he will yawn on command. There's no way I know of forcing a dog into a yawn, just patience and constant repetition of a word will teach him what you require. Every time Bracken yawned, I gave him the command Yawn. It only took him a few days before he associated the word with the action and will now do it to a hand signal as well as a verbal command. He loves showing off this new trick. When visitors come, he will sit in front of them and yawn. It's rather sad that most of the visitors don't realise how clever he's being and just think he's a tired dog.

I also taught him to look as if he's actually talking, opening and shutting his mouth and this came about purely by accident. I was trying to teach him to grin and show his teeth. I began by just giving him a word every time he opened his mouth. Originally I used the command Grin because this is what I intended to teach him, but it never came into a full grin. It ended up with him sitting and opening and closing his mouth. Now he would make a marvellous ventriloquist's dummy.

I have often embarked on teaching him something that's turned out to be quite different. You must be open to suggestions from your dog. If you watch carefully and understand him well enough, you will know what to train him and what he will enjoy doing. I have tried teaching Katy tricks. After a month of trying to teach her to yawn on command I gave up. Yet she enjoys doing the competition obedience side of her work and loves doing heel work, scent and Send-Aways. So, apart from teaching her to speak on command, I have left the other side of the training to Bracken.

There are a million little things you can teach your dog. Just simple exercises like offering a paw can be a pleasure to your dog. As Bracken naturally offered a paw, I took the exercise a little further and taught him which paw was which. For example, if I ask him for his right paw, he will offer that. It's simple enough to teach. Just take hold of your dog's paw gently and hold it up for him, praising him and giving him a command, 'Where's your paw?' Once he's got the idea, you can then tell him which paw is which. Right paw! and Left paw! repeated often enough and your dog will understand the words.

I am always trying to think of new things to train Bracken and, at the moment, I am teaching him his favourite trick in reverse. He loves taking rubbish out of the litter bin and bringing it to me. I am now showing him how to put rubbish into the litter bin. This exercise can only be taught if your dog really loves carrying and fetching things for you. Start off with an article that's easy to hold, like an empty cigarette box. Don't give him banana skins or orange peel, that will put him off. Try offering him your article. Some dogs prefer to pick up off the floor as they are used to doing this in their retrieve. As soon as your dog has the article in his mouth, run with him, with enthusiastic encouragement, giving the words, Bin it! As soon as you and the dog are at the bin, encourage him to drop the article and reward him with a titbit. You may have to do this a hundred times before your dog will take the initiative to go along on his own and drop the article in the bin. If he drops the article on the way, or outside the bin, don't scold him. It is a game. Forget it and start again. A little effort and enthusiasm on your part now could save you from getting up from your armchair in the evening to put your own rubbish in the bin. The dog will do it for you!

If your dog isn't interested in taking articles from you or picking them up from the floor, you can actually teach him to hold them, by gently placing the article in his mouth and stroking him under the chin, repeating the word Hold. This can also be the start of retrieve training if the dog refuses to pick up and bring back, but I have seen so much cruelty to dogs by owners who have rammed articles in the dog's mouth and held the jaws in a vice-like grip in order to prevent the dog from spitting it out. I do not wish to encourage any cruelty of that kind through my book, so let's keep all our training happy and lighthearted and move on to something else. If you find your dog does not like fetching and carrying for you, there are hundreds of

Bracken putting rubbish in the bin

other little tricks you can teach him. But the success or failure depends on your ability to understand your dog and to choose the right things for him. While every dog can be trained to be well-behaved and a pleasure to be with, they can't all be brilliant. Just like the human race, they have their attributes and failings.

CHAPTER 12

TRAINING THE OLDER DOG

It is far easier to train a young puppy, for the simple reason that bad habits have not developed. The older dog who has been undisciplined is just like an unruly child and will need far more time and firmness than a young puppy. The sad fact is that most owners do not train their dogs until they are older and have become complete lunatics. Where this has happened, the main aim is to gain complete control. In every case, there is the same basic problem, the dog has no respect for his owner. The easiest method of finding out whether your dog respects you or not is to praise him. If he comes to you with tail wagging and he's interested in what you have to say, he respects you. If he turns the other way when you stroke him and ignores you completely when you give enthusiastic endearments, he looks upon you as a doormat. All you have to do is to prove to him that you are not. Here are a few basic guidelines to follow if you own a disrespectful dog.

(1) Do not give your dog too much physical praise. Most dogs switch off when their owners stroke and pat them. And make him earn his verbal praise.
(2) Don't be afraid to speak your mind. That does not mean nag at him, but tell him when he's been a horrible dog and that you will not accept disobedience from him. Never yell this type of reprimand, but tell him in a low, disappointed tone.
(3) Never let him disobey you. If you say 'Sit', actually be there to put him into a Sit.
(4) Make sure you're giving your dog enough of your own time. Are you playing with him? Are you giving him enough exercise? There is nothing to make a big, active dog more disobedient than coiled-up energy.

All the basic training exercises can be done in your own kitchen, every spare minute during the day. One of the best and quickest ways of gaining your dog's respect is the 'bowl manners' technique, where you can assert your authority over the food bowl.

As with the puppy, you should sit your dog with his collar on, place the food bowl on the floor and hold the collar firmly, giving your dog the command Leave. Any form of disobedience or sign of aggression should be dealt with firmly but patiently. Don't be tempted to scream and yell at your dog, just tell him quietly that he must leave his dinner until you give him the command to Eat. As with a puppy, an older dog who is learning cannot be expected to wait very long for his dinner and a few seconds is perfectly acceptable for the first few days.

Teaching the dog to respond

Your dog must respond to you in the house. Make him understand that when you talk, he listens. Keep a soft leather collar around his neck in the day so you have some means of handling him easily. Call him to you often when you're around the house. If he ignores you, go up to him and take hold of his collar and bring him towards you, giving him the command Come. You will, of course, only be bringing him a foot or so, but then you must praise, not physically, but verbally, 'What a clever boy!' and hand out a titbit or a toy from your pocket. Repeated often enough, your dog will begin to understand that ignoring you is pointless and if he comes there will be a reward.

The boisterous dog

The leather collar will also be a very useful appendage when visitors call. Most untrained, older dogs delight in throwing themselves all over visitors and far too many owners side-step this training responsibility by shutting the dog in the kitchen. That is not the way to gain your dog's respect. Shut away, the average dog will get wound up and more excitable and determined that next time someone comes he will outwit you in his efforts to get to them before you can grab his collar and shut him away.

It is far better to take a little time and patience and train your dog to behave politely when visitors call. As soon as the doorbell rings and your dog hurtles down the hallway, barking furiously, pick up the lead, clip it on to his collar and tell him 'That will do!' Firmly put him in a Sit, and tell him to wait while you open the door. It would be advantageous if you could encourage a friend to come round in the initial training of this exercise, for it is very difficult to be struggling with your dog when a man comes to read the gas meter, or the milkman calls for his weekly dues. A friend may have a little more patience to hang around on the doorstep while you gain control of your lunatic. Having opened the door, your dog will no doubt lunge. Be ready for him with a good snatch on the lead and enforce your command and show him that you're very annoyed he's disobeyed. Put him back in the Sit and tell him to wait. If you need to repeat this twenty times, do so. Don't give up now to a life of shutting the poor dog away.

Once the dog is under control, invite your friend in. Ask her to give him just one stroke and a 'Good dog!' and from then on ignore him completely. Keeping the dog on his collar and lead, encourage the friend to sit down and make herself at home. Now, you must prove to the dog that you are in control. On no account must you let him launch himself at your visitor. Sit yourself down and make him lie at your feet. I feel it's a very good idea to train your dog to stay with you when visitors are around. If you can teach him that when anyone comes he's to stay by your chair rather than scuttle off to his bed in the kitchen, you have an added safeguard. That brush salesman could be a con-man. A dog that stays by you and looks the slightest bit protective could save you a lot of trouble. The con-man is hardly to know that, given a chance, your dog would leap all over him and lick him to death.

Of course, we are dealing with the over-friendly dog, but the same goes for the aggressive dog. For, as much as you need protection, you cannot afford to have a dog that will bite for no reason and you must therefore gain the same control. I know this sounds so simple but it will take you a long time to achieve a beautifully-behaved dog. But, with patience on your part, you will only need to instruct your dog to sit and wait at the sound of the doorbell—a collar and lead will not be necessary—and your visitors will admire your perfectly-behaved dog.

The older chewer

Chewing in the older dog can be a big problem, as the born chewer will set about his task of destruction when you're not around to correct him. Apart from the things that I have described with puppy chewing (leaving lots of things to amuse him if you're not around) you can take more defensive measures. For example, if he has a habit of chewing the wallpaper, coat the wall with mustard. This can often work, although I own up to the fact that I did this myself when Teak began to chew holes in the wood panelling. Far from deterring her, she was delighted the walls were coated with mustard and spent hours licking it off before proceeding to chew more holes. But you can experiment by sprinkling pepper or buying sprays for this purpose from your local pet shop. I might add here that it would be an advantage if you had mustard-coloured wallpaper! Not that it would make any difference to the chewing habits of your dog, but it would save you having unsightly blotches here and there. Or try the sit and wait method. You sit and wait where your dog cannot see you. Make all the preparations for going out as you would normally do, and having put your coat on, picked the shopping basket up, said goodbye to the dog and slammed the front door, creep back in and wait and listen. If you can hear any tearing noises from the other side of your kitchen door, now is your chance to rush in and grab hold of the dog by the scruff of the neck and give him a good shake. Tell him off for chewing the wallpaper or whatever. He'll be so shocked, if he was actually

Teaching the older dog to Sit
Rock the large dog backwards
with pressure on the collar and
ease the back down

fooled into believing that you'd gone out in the first place, he'll probably think twice about doing it next time. Although, here again, I must admit to you this method often fails, as the dog has such a keen sense of smell, he probably knows you're sitting on the other side of the door listening.

The barking dog

A similar method can also be used for the noisy dog who barks the moment you leave the house. But be careful how you handle this situation. Think about it for a moment. If you were a dog, you'd obviously be barking because you were lonely. If barking brought someone in, even to tell you off, you would do it just for the respite of that loneliness. So, a barking dog should be dealt with in reverse. By that, I mean you should only go in to him when he's quiet. If you can use the same technique, by waiting on the other side of the door and, after a few seconds' silence, go in and praise your dog. Barking should be met by a stern voice from the other side of the door, so that your dog realises he cannot achieve his ambition by making a noise, only by being silent.

I often get asked about barking or chewing dogs. First, I want to know all the circumstances in which the dogs are kept, and probably in seventy-five per cent of the cases it is the owners' doing. The dog is left locked up far too long while the owner goes out to work. The dog is not exercised enough, and does not have toys he can play with to occupy his mind. If you go out to work all day, it is mental cruelty to keep a dog locked up. An hour or two here and there is fair enough. Consider your dog. If you know you are going to be out for the whole morning, ensure that he's had plenty of exercise, even if it means getting up an hour earlier. My dogs, having had an hour's run in the woods from eight till nine in the morning, will sleep soundly until after lunch. A very active dog can be provided with something to keep his interest just before you leave home—a large marrow bone, a hide chew or his box full of toys. It's so easy to think your dog should behave—after all, you're only going out for an hour or two. But think of it from his point of view, he's not an adult, he doesn't have your type of reasoning power, he's equivalent to a young child. What would you do if you were a young child left alone in a house? I am sure that you wouldn't get into your bed and go to sleep and accept the fact. To be perfectly honest, I think most dogs are paragons of virtue, when you consider what they have to put up with from us human beings.

The unclean dog

It is most infuriating to have an adult dog who is unclean in the house. It is very simple to cure this habit, if you are there, by following the instructions given for house-training a puppy. The difficulty occurs when the dog is unclean when left alone at night or in the owner's absence in the daytime. There is not one single answer to this problem. There are many different reasons why your dog could be fouling the house. First of all, you must ensure that your dog is fit and healthy. If he's spending pennies far too frequently, then a visit to your vet is of paramount importance. If you are absolutely sure there is nothing wrong with your dog's health then various other things could account for his lapses. An entire dog will often cock his leg in the house to mark his territory, especially if there's a bitch in season close by. Castration is the answer here, as long as your dog is not too old. Otherwise, try spraying his favourite places with very strong smelling disinfectant.

A bitch's house-training will often be forgotten when she is coming into season and many bitches are ill on the approach and during their season. This must be accepted and it would be cruel to chastise the bitch in these circumstances. It would be far better to discuss this with your vet. If you have no intention of breeding with her then you can either have her spayed or put her on the Pill.

For a dog who fouls the house during the night, it is worth reviewing his diet. You may be giving him too much food. A dog of a year old and over should be receiving one meal a day. Titbits and little extras in between could be giving him tummy upsets. Do remember all dogs are different and whereas one type of food will suit one dog, it may not suit another. Experiment with different types of tin food, fresh meat or raw tripe. This may be your answer. Times of feeding could also play a big part in your dog's digestive system. It takes around twenty-four hours for a meal to pass through your dog. Most people tend to feed their dogs in the evening. Try feeding your dog early morning or lunch time to see if this has the desired effect.

CHAPTER 13

BEHAVIOUR OUTSIDE

The pulling dog

With an adult dog who pulls, you may need to resort to the use of a check-chain. The problem is that if a dog is left to pull, his neck muscles will become well developed and he'll become hardened to the collar around his neck and a week or two on a check-chain collar will bring him into line, *if used correctly*. The only reason check-chain collars are cruel is because of the ignorance of the users. Letting someone use a check-chain collar who is untrained is tantamount to giving a child a catapult. It can be very dangerous. If you stick rigidly to the guidelines below you should not make mistakes.

(1) The most important thing is that the check-chain must be worn by the dog correctly. I would think that fifty per cent of owners using check-chains put them around the dog's neck the wrong way.
(2) The check-chain should never be tight around your dog's neck.
(3) When wearing a check-chain, your dog should never be allowed to put his weight into the collar and pull.
(4) The correct type of check-chain is that of very small round links. The larger, oblong or oval type of links will stick when in use. The smoother the chain, the freer it will run; but don't use something too fine as this will cut into your dog's neck.
(5) Be absolutely sure that you know how to use the chain before putting it on your dog.
(6) Never, ever leave a check-chain on a dog in the house, or when he's free running. I know of dogs who have been choked to death by a check-chain.
(7) It is essential that the dog walks on your left hand side if you put the check-chain on correctly as shown.

I hope I have now made you realise how dangerous a check-chain can be if

Lead Training
TOP LEFT The most comfortable way to hold the lead
TOP RIGHT Let your arm be flexible
LEFT Correcting the dog

used incorrectly and I would always favour the half-check. But, for those of you who have large, very uncontrollable dogs, then I will explain how to use the check-chain correctly.

It is better to try out this new exercise in your garden, where your dog will not be too boisterous or trying to drag you to get to the next lamp-post. Give your dog a nice loose lead so that he can get at least a foot away from you. Hold the lead in your left hand. The placing of your left hand is very important, as pulling upwards or backwards will only give you shoulder-ache and will not train your dog. It is far more comfortable and effective to carry your lead with your left hand to the front of your hip. You can then flick your wrist upwards or, if necessary, take your hand across the front of your body. Timing is the most important thing when controlling the dog on a

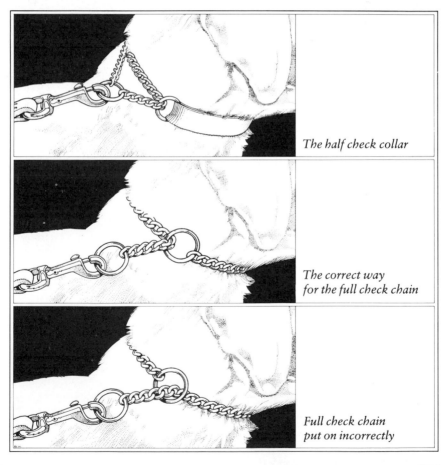

The half check collar

The correct way
for the full check chain

Full check chain
put on incorrectly

check-chain. Once the dog is pulling and has his full weight into the collar, you cannot use the check-chain correctly. The harder you pull and the dog pulls, the tighter the chain becomes. That is not the object of the exercise. You should get a feeling for the lead, and the moment that you feel the slightest bit of tension is the time to use the lead by a quick flick of the wrist, which will take the check-chain in and release it immediately. You must use your command with the action. Actions must go with words. The command Steady must be used at exactly the same moment the check-chain collar is tightening and loosening. If the dog has managed to get his full weight into the collar, you can then let your hand out to go with him to loosen the collar and then flick back. This must be done within a split second, otherwise your dog is lunging out with the little leeway you have given him. The action you are giving should not be a pull or a drag. I feel it's best described as a snatch. You snatch the lead.

Check-chain training the older dog can be a very arduous and time-consuming task but if you leave it, it will only get worse. Choose a nice quiet area to take your dog out for the first time with his check-chain, so you do not have to worry about passing dogs or busy pavements. It will not take one or two snatches of the lead, but hundreds with a really hard dog. You must have great determination and time to take him on long pavement walks. A ten minute walk here or there will only make him more excitable. It is far better to give him at least half an hour's pavement walk and check-chain training once or twice a day. Choose your times carefully. It is pointless to go out on a tight time schedule. You will be harassed and over-excited and tend to scream at your dog. This is the worst thing you can do. You must be in a relaxed mood and feel, at the start of your walk, however long it takes you, that you will stop your dog pulling by the time you reach home again. For the really bad pulling dog, perhaps you'd better take a packed lunch, tea and supper as well! Remember, it isn't strength that you need to control your dog, but speed. I often take five dogs out together. The weight and strength of my five dogs must far outweigh mine but I can control them easily by watching, being one step ahead of them. I don't watch the surroundings, as I can't see that far, so I keep an eye on my dogs, watching for telltale signs. Alert ears and a stiff tail can indicate the approach of a strange dog. A word of command from me, such as Leave, reminds them that I am on the other end of the lead and they must be on their best behaviour.

Exercising so many dogs at once reminds me of driving a car. You might be a good driver but you must always be on the alert for the lunatic behind the wheel. This is how I feel with my dogs. They can be under control and well-behaved but I must always watch out for the lunatic behind the lead, for it is always the owners to blame, remember that! Don't blame your dog. That's just as silly as blaming a car for careless driving.

The chaser

My heart aches when an owner comes to me with a chasing dog. 'I daren't let him off,' they tell me. 'He chases bikes, postmen, cars, children, other dogs.' Again, we have a situation where the poor dog suffers because the owner cannot be bothered to train against these things. I have heard so many remedies for the dog chaser which, in my opinion, would only make him worse. Many of these so-called remedies take the control of the dog out of the owner's hands and put the onus on the thing that's being chased. A good example of this is the dog who chases bikes. Two of the most frequently-used remedies are that the rider of the bike carries a jug or cup of water which he throws at the dog on his approach, or the rider of the bike offers the dog a titbit. If I were a dog and I had water thrown at me every time I approached a bike, I would hate them all the more and probably store up my vengeance and begin to recognise when a bike rider was carrying something in his hand. Dogs are intelligent enough to work that out, believe me. The second remedy, well, what would you do if you were given a titbit every time you ran after a bike? You'd do it all the more, of course. It is the owner of the dog who must gain control, not other people.

Control cannot be gained on just one exercise, as so many people think. 'All I want to do,' they tell me, 'is to get my dog to return when he's off the lead.' As soon as I suggest that control must be built up slowly and carefully over every training exercise, they decide to go somewhere else for help. I am offering them far too much hard work. If your dog will not respond to your command when he's chasing a cat out of the garden, there's no chance he'll respond in the park. It goes without saying that if you have trained correctly, your dog will return immediately or drop into a Down position as he's running away from you. So it is worth your while to read those chapters on Send-Aways and Fast Downs and Recalls.

The older dog will obviously be more difficult to train, so you must keep to the long lead training when you're in the park. You must be the deterrent to him chasing things. Once he's set out on his run, be ready to give that snatch as he gets to the end of the lead, along with a command of Leave. As soon as you've stopped him and are bringing him back, put enthusiasm into your voice. Tell him what a good boy he is. Reward him with a titbit and a game. Be patient. You will not change his habits overnight, it will take days, weeks, even months. But, be determined to be the boss. Prove to your dog that he can never get his own way and that you have control twenty-four hours a day.

Only when your dog responds to the Leave and Come commands time after time can you take off the long lead and, with a dog who has not been trained from a puppy, you may often need to revert to your long lead training, maybe once or twice a week. Even the best trained dogs need reminding of their lessons. The top competition obedience dogs are usually trained every day. Guide-dogs are working every day and, therefore, it is a type of training to them. You can't expect your dog to respond and to remember your training if you only take him out once a week. He will need his long lead training two or three times a day for long-lasting and effective results. There are some dogs who will constantly try to outwit you and gain leadership of the pack. You need a strong character and great determination to control a dog of this temperament.

Out of my five dogs, Buttons falls into this dominant category. The dominant dog may suit many people, although they don't suit me. I much prefer the more easy-going, submissive type of dog. Even on a lead, Buttons is looking for the opportunity to outwit me, if only to bark at a passing dog, or to grab a piece of stale bread off the pavement. My reactions to her have to be fast and firm but, having bought Buttons at a year old, at a time when I had a lot more to learn about the character and training of dogs, it is my duty to do the best I can and to try and change my temperament to suit hers. Having told you these things, I can also assure you that I could take Buttons anywhere and she would be on her best behaviour because of my constant training and reminders to her that I am in control.

CHAPTER 14

WE ALL MAKE MISTAKES

We all make mistakes, but do we learn by them? I certainly have learnt by the many mistakes I have made with dogs and I would like to tell you about the biggest mistake I have ever made. There may be dog trainers who think they know everything. These are the people to avoid, for if they have not had problems or made mistakes, they cannot understand other people's difficulties and, after all, nobody's perfect.

A couple of years ago, we had a space in our dog population. Rather than treat myself to another Labrador, I bought Don a breed I knew he fancied. I don't wish to tell you what breed Heidi was, as I feel this would prejudice you against the breed. Far too many people read a little of a wrongdoer—a biter or a chaser or a so-called untrainable dog—and label the whole breed with those attributes. I think that's very unfair. No breed is all bad or all good and I will not accept the responsibility of Heidi's breed suffering through my mistake, as I make no bones about it—it was my fault.

Heidi joined us at fourteen weeks of age, far too old. I hadn't seen the litter, I hadn't chosen her. I just picked her up from a dog show and although I wasn't enamoured of Heidi, I knew Don would be. Maybe in time, I told myself in the car journey home, I will like her. Don was delighted with his present, but the other five dogs were definitely not. At the tender age of fourteen weeks, Heidi was big and very dominant. House-training was my first problem with her. No matter how long I stayed in the garden and ensured that she 'spent her penny', she would always return into the house and find some more 'pennies to spend' on the kitchen floor. I attribute this to her living in a kennel until she came to us, when she was far too old, in my opinion, to begin house-training. Although it took me three months, at last I succeeded in having a clean Heidi. She was a very affectionate dog and I knew that all she longed for was constant human companionship. I didn't have the time, nor was I prepared to give her this. Although I hate admitting it to you, I feel I must be honest and tell you that I did not much like Heidi. I could not love her, and her little antics, which may have been a pleasure if Katy had done them, were annoying to me. Whines from Katy may have brought sympathy from me but whines from Heidi were excruciating. She sounded like a car eternally screeching to a halt. I tried every method I knew of stopping this habit but nothing worked and I realise now it was my lack of understanding of her character and needs that caused the problems between us.

It was obvious that Heidi did not like living with other dogs and was constantly vying for the leadership, not only of the canines but also of the humans in our home. I had never dealt with this total domination factor in a dog before. Many breeds of dogs will form a pack if more than two or three live together. This is not true of Labradors, who do not seem to worry about pack leadership. As a breed, they are quite happy to live together as a group, without trying to prove who is boss. Although Buttons is our most dominant dog, she has never tried to lead the others or put them in their place. Although I prefer a more submissive dog, the dominant type of animal can be very rewarding. I am convinced that if Heidi had been our first and only dog, we would have been thrilled with her. She was far more intelligent than any of our other dogs. An intelligent, dominant dog is a rarity and should be cherished if in the right hands. I always try to match canine characteristics with those of a human being. If you have some understanding of dominance and intelligence in people then you can relate it to a dog. There are many intelligent and learned people but, because they have the lack of drive or dominance, will probably never be anything special.

So it is with a dog. Heidi had completely the wrong characteristics to fit in with our home. She was quite unprepared to accept the way of life. Having so many dogs, there must be discipline. The dogs must conform to a regular routine: out in the morning for a good hour's run, asleep until lunchtime, out in the garden to play in the afternoon and then have dinner, back in the dog room to sleep until early evening, when the whole house is thrown open to them until bedtime. Heidi would not conform to this regime. As a puppy, she was not left in the dog room for hours on end, but given the attention allotted to all my puppies; lots of time for play and training and visits to the garden. She was only put in the dog room to have her sleep, which she seemed able to manage without.

My next problem was getting her to return, once off the lead in the park. Labrador puppies never want to run away and, when taken out at a very young age and let off the lead, they will only follow me. Heidi was completely different. I foolishly thought that if I took her to the park with the other dogs she would follow the others. I should have known better. The moment she was free she fled. I didn't make the same mistake twice. The next time, I took her out alone with a long training lead and began the arduous task of gaining an instant response on the recall. It took six weeks before I could totally trust Heidi off the lead.

I set about her basic training with great enthusiasm. There was no disputing her intelligence, she was far above the Labradors in brain power. But she wasn't very keen to use her intelligence on my training exercises.

With five dogs on the lead total control is imperative. If they all pulled at once I would take off!

She wouldn't accept titbits from me, she wouldn't play with me and resisted my every efforts to put her into a Sit or a Down. I hate using brute force when training a dog and will always try every other method first. I was beginning to think that brute force was the only thing left to me with Heidi, until I took one of the other dogs with me for the training lesson and showed her that it could be fun. By demonstrating with Katy, playing, accepting titbits, doing her training, etc, Heidi began to look upon this with a different view. She wanted the titbits and the toy for herself and I managed to persuade her to come round to my way of thinking, although it was not easy. I did manage to train Heidi to walk correctly on the lead, to sit and stay, down and stay and recall but, despite the fact that she was obedient—I would never let her be otherwise—there was always an undercurrent between us.

Heidi was never very fond of the other five dogs and she positively hated any strange dog that approached her and would scream at them with dislike and threaten them with blue murder if they so much as sniffed a hair on her body. At the tender age of nine months, she towered above all our dogs and regarded everything in and around the home as her sole possession to be guarded and I could feel aggression growing in her towards the other dogs. I could not face the prospect of constantly separating one dog from the next in case of fights. Our five dogs had always lived in peace until Heidi came. I discussed this problem with Don, who, like myself, was a little reluctant to face the truth of the matter that Heidi did not fit. She was our dog and our responsibility. A dog is not just for a few months but should be for life and that's what Don and I told each other frequently. But, as sure as I know there will be a tomorrow, I knew Heidi would strike. Her first victim was Buttons.

While my five dogs played happily in the garden together in the afternoon, Heidi never would. She stalked round them, occasionally giving a nip or a snarl at one of them. They all did their very best to ignore her. Then, one afternoon, for no apparent reason, Heidi picked Buttons up by her throat and was just in the process of throwing her on her back as I reached them to prevent any lasting injuries. Buttons was terrified, something very rare in her dominant character. She crept off to a corner and lay down and was afraid to move. I knew, without a doubt, Heidi's next victim would be Teak. Heidi followed Teak about the garden like a silent shadow, waiting for the right moment to attack. Teak would not crawl off into a corner, she would retaliate and, I feared, would have come off worse. She was much smaller than Heidi, and far less determined.

There were times when Heidi tried this silent stalking on me but I had the wit to turn and face her. She hated to be stared at, so would immediately turn and walk away. The strange thing about this dominance was Heidi's relationship with Kerensa. I was afraid for a while that Heidi would try and dominate her and, being at the tender age of five, she seemed a likely victim.

And yet, Heidi and Kerensa had something going for them. They played together in the garden for hours and Heidi loved the companionship of my young daughter and would willingly succumb to being led about the garden and even obey Kerensa's commands of Sit and Stay. In my experience, it is the dominant dogs who are best with children. They seem to understand that they are defenceless and are always on the alert to protect their young family. Buttons is certainly the most trustworthy of our dogs with young children. The more likely dogs to bite children are the very sensitive, submissive type of dog, who will bite from fear, not aggression.

The dog room at night became deserted as, first, we took Buttons out, for fear Heidi would attack her during the small hours. She joined Bracken in the lounge. Then Teak was taken out for the same reason. Heidi was left with Mocha and Katy. When I lay in bed at night I began to have fears that a scene of devastation would meet me in the morning, that Heidi would have turned on Mocha or Katy. These fears grew so strong that I had to tell Don about them. I was very reluctant at first because Heidi was his dog and I never like admitting defeat, but he agreed that he, too,. worried about Mocha and Katy. We both realised it was impossible to continue. We had the choice of parting with our five dogs and keeping Heidi, or parting with Heidi.

The choice was obvious. Heidi had to go. She was our responsibility and we had to weigh up all the pros and cons of finding her a new home. We knew she was not happy living with us—she hated sharing her home with other dogs, and wanted human beings to herself.

Our decision was not made lightly and, after a month or two of careful thought, we decided our only option was to find Heidi a home where she would be happy. Luckily, we had quite a choice and found someone who'd had a dog of Heidi's breed and was quite happy to take her on at almost a year old. Despite the fact there was no love lost between us, I was very sad to hand Heidi over to a new home. But, above my sadness was guilt. I had failed. I had admitted defeat. Looking back now, not emotionally involved, it was the best thing we could have done for her, for seeing her a few months after going to her new home, she was a different dog. She had changed from being neurotic, wound up, noisy, to a calm, self-assured, beautiful-looking animal and her owner could speak no wrong of Heidi's behaviour. They suited each other perfectly.

Another story I would like to tell you, in reverse, in the hope that it will give you a clearer understanding of how different dogs are and how important it is that you have the right dog for your family and way of life. I'm always very careful when I sell my Labrador puppies and I breed very rarely because of the worry and responsibility of finding the right home for the right puppy. I had a family waiting for a chocolate dog puppy for almost two years. At long last, a chocolate Labrador dog puppy came available for them. I was as sure as anyone could be that this was the right family for my puppy. He was just the right temperament for a family who had not owned a dog before. They were very keen and I spent an hour or two instructing them on his upbringing and training.

Within the first few weeks of his leaving home, I wasn't satisfied with the response from my telephone calls to his new family. They were constantly niggling about little things he did. 'He bit the children,' I was told. On closer questioning, the puppy was not actually biting the children but trying to play tug-of-war with their slippers or tugging at their nighties. 'He won't obey all the time,' they said. 'Sometimes he sits and sometimes he doesn't.' I tried to explain to them that such a young puppy needed constant reminders and was not likely to learn our English language within the first fortnight.

I was beginning to think I must have been wrong about this puppy's temperament. As soon as I realised all was not well I took the puppy back. But much to my amazement, I was right in my original assessment. He was very easy to train. I could hardly believe that even a six-year-old couldn't have coped with him. He was a positive delight and within a fortnight, at the age of twelve weeks old, I had him doing a Sit-Stay, a Down-Stay, walking nicely on the lead, a recall and obeying all the household words. Needless to say, I would love to have kept this puppy but Bracken wouldn't have been very keen on another male sharing his home. Luckily, I always have one or two people waiting for chocolate puppies and I was able to find him another home close at hand, so that I could keep my eye on him. He settled immediately and was never any problem.

After this experience, I am even more reluctant to breed puppies. Each time I've bred and sold a litter, I've felt ten years older!

A Dog's Dream

CHAPTER 15

MONGRELS

Many people prefer mongrels to pedigrees. I have no preference. The fact that I own Labradors is because of Emma. But I would be just as eager to own crossbreds if we had more room and money. I did own a mongrel for a week and I would have loved to have kept her, but at the time we had Heidi, and Heidi definitely did not like our little mongrel. I came upon Solo purely by chance. My local pet shop does not stock live animals, so I feel quite safe in shopping there. But one day, as luck would have it, I went shopping with a friend who owned a car, so we decided to be a little more adventurous and go further afield. Just like a dog, when it comes to passing pet shops, I can't do it—I have go to in. The first thing I spotted was Solo, a tiny black crossbred puppy, all alone, in a cage which was far too small. I knew without a shadow of doubt that I couldn't leave her there. To my horror, she was only £5. The shopkeeper asked me no questions and gave me no information whatsoever about how to feed or care for this little puppy. I was horrified. Pet shops make it far too easy for the impulse buyer and so many of the puppies bought on the spur of the moment are discarded within a month. She was far smaller than a Labrador puppy and very different in temperament. She was shy and retiring and didn't live to eat! All the dogs, except Heidi, viewed her with kindly curiosity. Heidi threatened to kill her. I installed Solo in a covered-over cat basket. She squeezed herself right to the back and refused all offers of food. All through this procedure my dogs lay around the basket in a circle licking their lips, hoping for a chance of the food this silly puppy was refusing. My heart went out to her as she seemed so afraid of these monsters that patrolled around her basket. Whenever Heidi passed Solo tried to bury herself under the blanket. As much as I wanted this little puppy, I knew it was impossible, for at the time Don and I were still wrestling with our consciences as to whether Heidi should go or not, and as Heidi was Don's dog I felt it was very unfair to push her out so that I could keep this little puppy. Instead, I rang everyone I knew to tell them about her and asked for their help in finding her a suitable home. I gave very careful thought to the type of home which would suit Solo. She was a very sensitive little puppy but I knew that with the right handling and environment she would make someone a marvellous pet. I was very fortunate in finding her a home locally with no young children or other dogs. She blossomed into a delightful little dog. She looks somewhere

between a Labrador and a collie in miniature. She has repaid her family a thousandfold for the care and attention they have lavished on her. Even if she is only a little mongrel she has become a pleasure to be with and a winner at the Obedience shows.

I know of many who have visited our local dog shelters and brought home a mongrel. Some of the relationships have worked, others, sad to say, have not and the dogs have been returned. The major fault when choosing a mongrel is that everyone goes on looks. I don't advocate you have a dog that you don't like the look of, but it's far easier to live with a horrible-looking dog who has a super temperament than with a handsome dog with a nasty streak. Just because you are choosing an unwanted mongrel from the local dogs' home does not mean you should disregard your temperament and requirements and the dog should be chosen just as carefully as if you were choosing a pedigree puppy of great value. If you have children then it is essential that they come with you because your first requirement in this case is a dog that will get on well with your children. It is essential that you speak to someone at the shelter who has been caring for and feeding the dogs and will have some idea of the temperament and characteristics of the dogs in their charge. Some dogs may have background information if they have been brought in by their owners but many will have just been found abandoned. The following list of questions may help you to evaluate the temperament of the dog:

(1) Does the dog growl when his food bowl is put down? If so, he's dominant.
(2) Does he bark a lot? If so, he's excitable.
(3) How does he greet the kennel maid—always tail wagging, a little suspiciously or growling? The dog who greets with a wagging tail is obviously outgoing and friendly. The suspicious dog may be worried he's in strange surroundings with people he doesn't know. He may be the type of dog who gives loyalty to a family and isn't interested in strangers. The dog who growls may do so for two different reasons—he's very dominant and plain nasty, in which case move along. But he may growl because he's absolutely terrified and if you particularly want this dog it may be worth your while sitting with him, talking to him and noting his responses. After a minute or two he may come up to you and accept your praise. If he huddles in a corner and bares his teeth he's obviously had some very nasty experiences and it's touch and go whether you will make it together.

Having narrowed the field a little with these questions you can then go back to the dogs you think will be suitable for you. If you have children, introduce them and note the reaction. Spend a little time with each dog. Maybe he's too friendly for you with tail wagging and leaping up and down. The exuberant dog will suit an exuberant owner. You may not be cut out to deal with this type of characteristics. Your final test should be putting the dog on a collar and lead and taking him for a walk. Is he aggressive to the other dogs he passes on the way through the kennels? A quiet dog may become a lunatic on the end of a lead once out on the pavement. You must not accept the dog because you feel sorry for him, things must be right all along the line for you to have a long and happy relationship. There are hundreds of dogs to choose from. Don't just have a dog for the sake of it. Be prepared to visit other dog shelters, or to return weekly until your ideal dog turns up. Remember, if a lot of thought and care had gone into choosing these puppies in the first place they wouldn't be abandoned. You must be one hundred per cent convinced that the dog you choose will stay with you for the rest of his life.

CHAPTER 16

DOG TRAINING SHOULD BE FUN

Don't fall into the trap of many dog owners of forgetting the fun element in your training. If life with your dog has become a drudgery and the time you take to train him basic commands is full of harassment, fraught with anxiety, *stop*, you have got it all wrong. Dogs, like children, should be a pleasure to us. I see all types of human beings coming along to my training classes with their dogs and I can instantly tell you which ones will fall into the 'failed owners' category. They're the ones who won't listen, who won't try, who think they will make a fool of themselves talking to their dog and putting enthusiasm into their voices. Many of them refuse point-blank to sit on the ground with their dogs and think it childish and stupid to play with them. In my training classes I try and make most of the exercises a game so that the human beings forget their self-consciousness and before they realise it they are having as much fun as their dogs. It is very rewarding to train along with other people and their dogs, as it gives incentive to the owners to come out best. If you train with other people or go along to a training club perhaps some of these ideas will help you and if you're the stiff and starchy conservative type maybe it will give you enthusiasm to change your dog's training and have fun.

However many times I tell my class to be quick putting their dogs into a Sit at the Halt, their responses are slow and lethargic, until I turn it into a game. I get the handlers walking round in a circle, reminding them that this could be very boring for the dogs, so to give lots of encouragement and enthusiastic words. On my command of Halt, they must instantly put their dogs into a Sit. Dogs that are slow are eliminated, therefore ending up with the fastest dog and owner winning our Quick Sit competition. You'd be amazed how pleased these dog owners are to have won.

Our Fast Down game is done with three or four handlers at a time moving quickly down the field and imagining they are walking through a flock of sheep. I am the farmer and come out with a double-barrelled shotgun and any dog that is not in the Down position on my command of Down is

shot (not literally I hasten to add). Both humans and canines love this and I hear comments such as, 'Oh dear, my dog's been shot three times this week, I really must practice these Fast Downs at home,' but all the dogs' tails are wagging and the owners are smiling, especially those with 'live' dogs at the end of the exercise.

Our Stay exercise is made into a game. I think training Stays can probably be the most boring part of dog training and our owners again are instructed to leave their dog in a Stay while they run and touch an obstacle in the middle of the circle. If the dog gets up it is not met with bored lack of interest by the owner but is put back into its Sit-Stay with speed and alacrity so that the owner can fulfil the task. The dogs learn much quicker this way and the owner whose dog has failed in one week is determined it won't the next time the training lesson comes round.

The owners who seem to have the biggest problem are those owning boisterous, over-enthusiastic dogs, who leap about at the end of the lead on two legs, fervently believing that everything that moves is their best friend. These are the dogs who have my greatest sympathy, as their owners complain to me, 'He's totally out of control. I can't do a thing with him. He won't sit still for a moment at home and today he's dug half the lawn up.' If only these owners would stop and think about the temperament of their dog, and what he really needs from life. Training their dog could be so much fun, instead of constant nagging. It is an accepted fact that bright children are usually a handful, always wanting to do something, getting bored quickly. They desperately want to learn, but not in the old-fashioned way of sitting and swotting. These type of children need an entirely different approach. They love competitive sports and will knuckle down to do anything if enough praise and enthusiasm is given to them. And so it is with the over-enthusiastic dog. It is pointless yelling at him to stop pulling, or sit down or be quiet. The only training for this type of dog must be fast-moving, interesting and full of enthusiasm. These dogs are the ones who respond best to the Fast Down and Quick Sit games, in fact some of them are much faster than their owners. When I shout 'Halt' the dogs are sitting before their owners give the command. When I shout Bang in Fast Down games, these dogs drop like a stone. Around the house they need constant attention. If you want a happy, well-trained dog you must be prepared to spend time with your dog, playing with him, but remember the games should contain discipline. For example, you can do a few seconds Wait before playing his favourite ball game, and this type of dog will love hunt the sock. The more training exercises and tricks you can teach him the better. This dog will throw himself with great enthusiasm into pleasing you and learning new things. No matter how old your dog is or how well-trained, don't forget he needs rewards, lots of praise and titbits. I often get handlers who, after a

TOP *Training classes should be fun*
CENTRE *The dogs love Fast Sits*
BOTTOM *. . . and Fast Downs*

few months of attending the training class, tell me, 'I've stopped giving him titbits, he knows the exercises, and it's only bribery. He should do it for me, not for what he gets out of it,' they announce with characteristic human arrogance. The well-trained dog will carry out orders without being rewarded with titbits, my dogs do, but that doesn't mean to say I don't reward them for their efforts. Ask any wife how she feels, when her husband comes home with a bunch of flowers or a box of chocolates, it makes all the difference in the world just to feel one is appreciated and rewarded. Dogs are not machines, they need motivating, and a little kindness, love and reward goes a long way.

CHAPTER 17

WHERE HAVE YOU GONE WRONG?

Do you still have an uncontrollable dog? Then somewhere along the line you've gone wrong. I'll start right from the beginning. Chances are, if you've chosen your puppy before reading this book, you are not compatible and, after all, human beings do make mistakes—the divorce rate proves that. So how can we be naïve enough to believe that we will match every dog, and that our lives together will automatically be wonderful? You should take as much care choosing your puppy as you would in choosing your husband or wife. But what if everything has gone wrong and you feel you can't cope? If you love your dog, you will persevere, and I hope you will try to change your character and temperament to suit your dog. If, on the other hand, there is no love lost between you, then the kindest possible thing is to find your dog a more suitable home. This does not mean dumping him or taking him to the nearest animal shelter. He is your responsibility and you must see it through. You may think he's untrainable and a nuisance but someone else will undoubtedly find him a pleasure to live with. It's worth asking your local veterinary surgeon if he knows anyone who is looking for an adult dog. If you advertise in the papers, be very sure that you ask the prospective owners all the right questions. For instance, have they had a dog of this breed before? Is there someone at home to be with him? Are they willing to train and accept him, faults and all? There should never be any need to abandon your dog, as there are always plenty of good homes for the older dog. Don't be conceited enough to think that because you can't train your dog no one else can.

Having explained the worst that can happen, let us hope it doesn't, and that you wish to have a nicely-trained dog, however long and hard you must work to achieve this end.

Back to Basics

The biggest mistake most dog owners make is that they don't mean what they say. How often do we hear the screams of 'Sit! . . . sit! . . . *sit!*' while the owner stands there motionless. Actions must go with words. Each and every time you give the Sit command, be in a position to put your dog into the Sit. If you give a command without insisting it is carried out, the dog will remember. You, as well as your dog, must live by certain rules and regulations. It may be amusing to see your dog jump up in the kitchen and hang his nose over the sink, but it won't be so funny next day when he steals your freshly-baked cake from the table.

All the basic training should be carried out in the home or the confines of your garden, where you can ensure the dog is listening to you and obeys. Wherever you are in the house, try and incorporate little training exercises: waiting for the kettle to boil is an ideal opportunity to do a Sit-Stay, for example. Recalls should be carried out frequently, and never let your dog ignore you. If you call him and he doesn't appear, find him, bring him to you and offer a titbit and lots of praise. That way he's much more likely to respond to your command in the future.

Your dog will only be as good as you are in respect of your attitude and ability to train him. If you put him into a Sit slowly and hesitantly, that's how he will always carry out your commands. Everything must be done with firmness and speed, and don't forget your praise should be lavish and instant. Voice control is a great asset to dog training. Maybe you could practice this on a tape recorder. It is terrible listening to your own voice, I know, but it may give you some understanding of what your dog has to put up with. Try praising on the tape recorder and then follow with a command. See if you can tell the difference. If you can't, how do you expect your poor dog to understand? Orders should be given firmly, not shouted and yelled—otherwise our best dog trainers would be Sergeant Majors. And a 'Good boy' is not very interesting as far as your dog is concerned unless you can put great enthusiasm into your voice.

It is mutual understanding and respect that builds a loving relationship with your dog. Just like a marriage, keeping the partnership going is hard work. You must understand your dog and give time to his requirements—you can't expect him to be the one that gives all the time. You must ensure that he's exercised regularly and has plenty of free time—a dog who's cooped indoors all day is bound to be a handful and will resent your discipline because there is no freedom with it. A dog who isn't treated as one of the family will be more inclined to ignore your commands. A dog who's left at home on family outings because he's a nuisance will become much more of a nuisance. And the dog who's shut outside in a kennel stands little chance of being an obedient, loving companion.

TOP *Everybody out!*
BOTTOM *The dogs waiting for the command to eat*

I count myself very fortunate to have had a really good relationship with Emma. She was with me twenty-four hours a day and I understood her like I understood part of myself. I had to interpret the movements from the handle when she was working at my side and I had to understand her every little whim when she was off duty at home. A gentle nudge would be, I want to play, and a firmer push with the nose would indicate she wanted to go into the garden. Her little snorts or the way she bounced around me all indicated her needs or thoughts and, in the same way, she was able to interpret my feelings and moods. Although the type of relationship we had only comes once in a lifetime, if you're very lucky, I feel we should all aim for that perfection with our dogs.

Dog training, as with anything else in life, needs time and effort to reap its rewards, and dog ownership itself needs very careful thought. You would be amazed how many people who want to buy a puppy from me go out to work all day. These people—who call themselves dog lovers—are prepared to shut the dog in from eight o'clock in the morning to six o'clock at night. How would you feel if you were locked in a room every day with no one to talk to, with no company at all and not even toilet facilities for you? You would go mad, so why is it so strange that your dog becomes destructive, unclean and unresponsive when you treat him like this? On reflection, we human beings are a rotten lot. We expect everything from our dogs and give nothing in return. We use our canine friends for so many purposes and yet have still not acknowledged their true place in our society. On the one hand we expect them to be guide-dogs, while on the other we chop their tails off because it's fashionable. We have bred dogs so deformed or so odd in stature that they live a very short and unhappy life. I have seen, with horror, many top show or working dog kennels where the animals are kept in such appalling conditions that I could weep. Dogs are often left to lie in their own excreta, with no blanket or straw, driven to distraction by the lack of exercise or human companionship. This goes not only for the ambitious people who want to win in breed, obedience or field trials, but also for the irresponsible pet owner with ill-kept dogs chained up in the yard and ignored for a large part of their existence.

I am sure that if you have taken the time and trouble to read this book you are not one of the culprits, but it is so easy to fall into that category without realising it. Let's take a very simple example. You have bought a dog and despite the fact that you have spent time and effort training him, he still digs holes in your lawn, uproots the rose bushes and kills your best flowers by watering them frequently. You could easily become the sort of owner who says, 'I'm not letting that dog in my garden, he's ruining it—he'll have to be chained up.' Chain your average well-adjusted pet up in the garden and you will change his personality. Would you accept being chained up and left to pass the day away dreaming? I know I certainly wouldn't! I'd complain bitterly and shout until someone released me, and when they did I would go mad to release my pent-up anxieties and energy. If you are a garden-proud owner, either don't have a dog or change your gardening methods.

We did have quite a nice back garden before the onslaught of the dogs: lawns, flowerbeds, trees and a vegetable patch. The lawns were soon changed into muddy quagmires, the rose bushes were completely eliminated by Bracken, daffodils had their heads snatched off by playful puppies and the bean patch was regarded as the 'busy spot'. So Don, my husband, re-designed the whole thing so that it could accept dogs and still look nice. Our stretch of lawn is fenced off and the rest of the area is paved for cleanliness and neatness, with walled areas for flowers and tall pots to contain the more delicate growths such as fuschias and geraniums. The height of these pots was considered carefully, just a little bit taller than Bracken's leg could go. We not only have a nice neat garden, but Don has far less to do. A small strip of lawn to mow, and pots and walled gardens that can so easily be weeded at the weekends.

You probably aren't considering having five dogs to range about your homestead but even one dog can cause chaos to your well-kept garden so it's worth considering what you want before purchasing your dog.

Summing up

The whole basis of a good relationship rests on a good match. There is, somewhere, the perfect dog for you if you can spot him and then know how to handle him. It is very important, when applying any of the training lessons, that you understand the temperament of your dog. A very dominant dog will need firm handling and probably far more training. He will vie with you for leadership and probably defy your every wish. You must prove to him that you are boss. No matter how many times you put him into a Sit, you must repeat your physical actions over and over again until your dog beats you to it. You must have determination in your mind when training this type of dog. It may take you months to get an instant recall from him on your long training lead when out in the park, but you must persevere or you will end up with a disobedient dog for the rest of his life. And a disobedient dog is a very unhappy dog. Although the sensitive dog is more easily trained, they are also quickly ruined by hard handling. The sensitive dog will freeze with fear, unable to carry out a command. If this dog is misread, he will soon become a nervous wreck and may even bite out of fear. It is a sad fact that a majority of pet owners are unable to read the temperament of their dogs correctly and, even worse, they are unable to train them. You will know these people instantly when you meet them. They are full of excuses: 'I've been so busy lately, I haven't been able to take him out,' or, 'There must be a bitch in season somewhere, that's why he's badly behaved,' or, 'I just haven't had time for him since the baby came.'

In my opinion, there is no point owning a dog unless he's a pleasure to you and you are prepared to put hard work, time and effort into his training. It is not easy to train a dog and I do not believe it can be done in minutes. It takes months, or even years if you're aiming for perfection. But the pleasure of having an obedient and loving dog as a constant companion is immeasurable.